Cultivating Neighborhood

Cultivating Neighborhood

Identifying Best Practices
for Launching a Christ-Centered
Community Garden

BRYAN K. LANGLANDS

Foreword by
WILL WILLIMON

RESOURCE *Publications* · Eugene, Oregon

CULTIVATING NEIGHBORHOOD
Identifying Best Practices for Launching a Christ-Centered
Community Garden

Resource Publications
An Imprint of Wipf and Stock Publishers
199 W. 8th Ave., Suite 3
Eugene, OR 97401

www.wipfandstock.com

ISBN 13: 978-1-62564-656-9

Manufactured in the U.S.A.   08/22/2014

Scripture quotations are from:
The NEW REVISED STANDARD VERSION BIBLE, copyright ©1989
by the Division of Christian Education of the National Council of the
Churches of Christ in the U.S.A.

For Amanda, Ava, Vivienne and Hazel

Contents

Foreword

ACCORDING TO GENESIS, WE had our beginning in a garden. Life in a lush, fecund garden was God's originating intention for us. The first thing that God commanded us to do was to be gardeners. As with many of God's plans for humanity, things did not turn out as God intended. In our rebellion against God, in our determination to take matters into our own hands, to be dominators of the earth rather than co-creators with God, we desecrated the primal garden. We found ourselves cast out into the rocky, thorn-ridden desert where we were warriors against rather than cultivators of Creation and neighborhood. Isaiah prophesied a day when the Messiah comes, when the arid desert, the Creation we have desecrated, shall burst into bloom. One day, when God gets God's way with the world, the whole world shall again be God's good garden.

Thus, even in our wilderness, God did not desert us. Throughout the biblical story, God does some of God's best work in gardens. Jesus connected heaven and earth in his agricultural parables of seedtime and harvest, the mystery of seed sprouting and bearing fruit, the wonder of wheat, and the lilies of the field, the spiritual insight that comes with the seemingly mundane tasks of working the soil. One fateful night, Jesus did some powerful wrestling with God's will in Gethsemane's garden. Mary Magdalene mistook the risen Christ for a gardener, says John's gospel.

When we think about the story of Christ through the eyes of gardeners, Jesus' cross and resurrection, the heart of the Christian faith, is framed by gardens.

And yet I had never really thought much about connecting gardening with the Christian faith until I read Bryan Langlands' *Cultivating Neighborhood*. Bryan takes the metaphor of "cultivation" and couples gardening and local church life in a way that transformed my thinking and perhaps even changed my ministry. I had some experience in neighborhood, community gardening, and I am a pastoral leader of a congregation, but until *Cultivating Neighborhood* I had not put the two practices together theologically. This book makes an engaging case for, and then actually demonstrates how to make happen, the cultivation of neighborliness through a church sponsored garden.

Yet *Cultivating Neighborhood* is more than a manual for how churches can engage in gardening. It is also a spirited, gracious invitation to the changed congregational culture that occurs when churches risk linking our Christian beliefs to the practices of gardening. Bryan adeptly moves us from certain Christian ideals like neighborhood, community, and peacefulness to practices that cultivate these virtues in the everyday life of congregations. I am convinced after reading *Cultivating Neighborhood* that the fruit harvested through church gardening is of greater significance even than the delicious and wholesome home grown vegetables coming from the garden. Something there is within the Christian faith that makes gardening a fruitful practice for Christians as much as keeping Sabbath, tithing, Bible study and prayer.

Bryan not only manages to mount a theological rationale for why Christians and their churches should be focused upon gardening but also gives practical, step-by-step advice on how a congregation begins to make gardening in the name of Christ a part of their congregational life.

Pastors and church leaders will find wonderfully useful the case studies of actual congregations that dug into God's good earth. Bryan even ends the book with a checklist of what his congregation did in order to begin cultivating neighborhood through gardening.

We have here that rare Christian book that not only urges us on toward greater faithfulness but shows us how to get there.

Cultivating Neighborhood has convinced me of a wonderful truth: In cultivating a garden in the name of Christ, in reconnecting ourselves with the wonder of God's gracious provision for our sustenance through gardening, in joining with others to perform the tasks required in order to cultivate a garden, we find that God lovingly uses a basic human act like gardening to cultivate us to be more faithful lovers of God. Just what one ought to expect of a God who not only created the world as a garden before God created us, but also showed up to us as Jesus Christ, God with us – particularly present with us when we garden.

Will Willimon

Acknowledgments

I AM DEEPLY INDEBTED to a host of friends and colleagues who helped to make this book project possible. In the early stages, Lew Parks strongly encouraged me to pursue my ideas about creating a field-guide to help churches that might be interested in launching a community garden. Without that encouragement, this project would have never happened. Similarly, I would like to thank Amy Oden for her support, encouragement, and for her careful review of this manuscript. Her suggestions for improvement were tremendously helpful.

I am also grateful for the support and energy that the Kai Sunday School Class at Faith Baptist Church in Georgetown, KY brought as they helped me to start the Allelon Community Garden there. Since our very first conversations about the possibility of starting that garden, Jonathan and Elizabeth Sands Wise and Jeremiah Tudor have been constant and faithful friends, supporters and co-laborers. I would also like to thank Jeremy and Laura Colliver, Jeremy and Beth Sexton, and Matt Makaveli for helping to get Allelon started. Similarly, without the support and leadership of Pastor Bob Fox, Allelon would not have happened. And although her time with us at Allelon was short, our new friend Charlotte Schaut was a gift from God. If there is any gardening to be done in the rest of heaven, I trust that she is there, growing the greatest garlic imaginable. May she rest in peace.

Acknowledgments

Grace Hackney and Homer White were incredibly gracious in allowing me to interview them for this book. Their experience and wisdom with community gardening were invaluable. Just as their insights helped us as we were dreaming about starting Allelon, my hope is that others who are thinking about launching a Christ-centered community garden will be similarly inspired.

Finally, without the love and support of my entire family, none of this would have been possible. My prayer is that my three daughters will learn to love gardening with others as much as I have, and that God will reveal to them as many wonderful things as have been revealed to me through the inscrutable grace of having your hands in the soil.

Introduction

A Brief History of Community Gardening in the United States

IT HAS BEEN DOCUMENTED that in the United States since the final decade of the nineteenth century, interest in community gardening has spiked during times of social and economic crisis.[1] Variously, these occasions of social crisis have included times of war, economic depression, massive migration, political upheaval and popular movements of dissent, among others. This connection causes one to wonder *why* there has been a consistent-across-generations turn towards community gardening in the midst of social crisis? Whence the interest? And how specifically has the practice of community gardening served as a salve to heal the wounds of social crisis?

More recently, the first decade of the twenty-first century in the United States has witnessed an almost continuous stream of crisis events. From the tragic violence on September 11, 2001, to the subsequent military operations in Afghanistan and Iraq, to Hurricane Katrina in 2005, to the economic collapse of 2008

---

1. See Laura Lawson's critical history of community gardening in the United States entitled *City Bountiful: A Century of Community Gardening in America* (Berkeley, CA: University of California Press, 2005).

and the subsequent economic recession/depression, to the swine flu frenzy of 2009, the previous decade has been rife with crisis. Given the research mentioned earlier, it should come as no surprise that the previous decade has also witnessed an explosion in interest in community gardening. But what has marked this most recent explosion in community gardening as distinctive is the fact that so many *churches* have launched community gardens over the past decade. One is left to wonder why it is exactly that *churches* have taken it upon themselves to start community gardens? What is the relationship between social crisis, churches and the growth of church-sponsored community gardens in the United States over the past decade?

Hopefully, what follows will begin to offer some answers to these important questions. But before one can delve too far into the specifics of church-sponsored or Christ-centered community gardens (part of the task of this project will be to distinguish between the two), it is necessary to decipher what, exactly, a community garden is. Indeed, church-sponsored and Christ-centered community gardening are subsets of the larger movement in the United States of community gardening (sometimes known as urban gardening). Understanding the larger historical and cultural horizons out of which recent iterations of church-sponsored community gardening have appeared will enable connections to be made between past developments and the present.

In what follows, first I will briefly trace out the concept, history and some generally desired outcomes of community gardening in the United States. Then, I will turn towards the culture of the church in recent years to unpack what issues and situations in the church may have led to the recent surge in interest on the part of churches and church-based institutions in launching community gardens. Next, a hypothesis regarding that interest will be proposed. After fleshing out constructively a thick conception of *gospel hospitality* that might underwrite our practices of Christ-centered community gardening, I will offer two case studies of church-sponsored community gardens (Anathoth Community Garden in Cedar Grove, NC and Allelon Community Garden in Georgetown, KY) and one case study of a community garden launched by a Christian college (Georgetown College in Georgetown, KY). Each of these three gardens has been launched within the past nine years. Hopefully, each of these case studies will help the reader to understand the reason why each garden was created, the challenges each one faced and the successful strategies that were used. This book will conclude with suggestions for best practices in launching a Christ-centered community garden.

To commence, then, what is a community garden? And what is the relationship of community gardens to urban gardens? Basically, a community garden is a portion of land that is farmed by a group of people. In her book *City Bountiful: A Century of Community Gardening in America*, Laura Lawson traces the roots of present-day community gardening back to the vacant-lot gardening programs of the 1890s in the Northeast in which the poor (especially recent immigrants) were encouraged to garden and/or instructed in the basics of gardening. Following those urban gardening beginnings, Lawson describes the school garden movement, the War Garden Campaign during World War I, garden programs during the depression of the 1930s, the Victory Garden Campaign during World War II, and the development of the community garden movement in the 1970s and 1980s. She concludes with a section on urban garden programs from 1990 to the present and a look at community gardens today. Interestingly, in this book (which was published in 2005) Lawson does not mention church-sponsored community gardens. The reason for this silence is because in 2005 church-sponsored community gardening was still in its infancy and, unlike today, hardly discernible as a national trend.

Given this tradition of community gardening in the United States, one wonders why so many generations have found community gardening to be a beneficial thing? What, after all, is the *good* of community gardening? Perhaps the important prior question that needs to be asked would be, what is the good of *gardening itself*? Indeed, regardless of whether one is working in a backyard garden, a company garden, a school garden or a community garden, Lawson reports,

> To many people, the act of gardening felt good physically and emotionally. As a diversion or hobby, gardening relaxed people and helped to soothe the tensions inherent in busy lifestyles. While most gardeners could anecdotally claim that gardening was therapeutic and restorative, this connection between gardening and mental health received a boost from scientific study in the 1970s. Environmental psychologist Rachel Kaplan's 1973 study showed that gardening and viewing green spaces produced a restorative response. Including both community gardeners and home gardeners as subjects, her research found that people enjoyed gardening for the experiences it provided, such as working the soil, seeing things grow, learning new things about gardening, and being outside. In addition, gardens provided sustained diversion, aesthetic pleasure, an opportunity to relax, and a sense of accomplishment. The tangible results – the tilled earth, the food produced, beautiful flowers – also contributed to the satisfaction and restoration that people found in gardening.[2]

Thus, garden participants describe many different kinds of experiential goods connected to gardening. But how do these goods connect with the goods and goals of community gardening?

Surely, the goods mentioned above related to gardening in general would carry over to the goods and desired outcomes for most community gardens. In addition to those goods, community gardens typically set out larger goals that have something to do with the strengthening of (or in some cases the creation of) a community of people. Although distinctions exist between the *raisons d'être* and goals for different iterations of urban/community gardening, there are also overlaps and congruities of purpose among them. For example, when Lawson mentions several possible objectives for community gardening moving forward into the future, her list includes such goals as growing food, recreation, education,

2. Lawson, *City Bountiful*, 217.

economic opportunity, and environmental restoration (among others).[3] This list could also function broadly as a list of common objectives for community gardening historically (although instead of "environmental restoration," urban garden proponents historically would have probably spoken of "beautification"). Such a list helps one to see in broad terms what the goods of a community garden are.

Of course, each iteration of urban/community gardening has had its own peculiar emphases regarding objectives. One thinks, for example, of the vacant-lot cultivation programs and their goals of assimilating recent immigrants into the culture of American agrarianism, etc., and the Victory Gardens of World War II as freeing up labor for the war-production industry.[4] Similarly, when corporations began looking at the possibility of creating company gardens, they were looking at the ways in which these gardens might help their bottom lines. The rationale was that allowing workers to garden helped their mental health, their physical health, and their employee satisfaction. In an address to the National Victory Garden Conference, E.J. Condon, assistant to the president of Sears, Roebuck and Company, once stated that,

> Company gardens make for excellent employee relations. Nerves in a war plant get pretty threadbare. The noise, the strain and the constant pressure make for short tempers. Take a couple of riveters off the assembly list. Put a hoe in their hands and put them into a garden patch. It's just plain good for a man's soul.[5]

Indeed, many corporations noted connections between the health that gardening fosters, healthy employees and increased productivity.

More recently, the American Community Gardening Association drafted a vision statement around the year 2000 that speaks

3. Ibid, 294–7.
4. See Lawson, Chapters 1 and 6.
5. Lawson, *City Bountiful*, 185.

in contemporary terms to the common goods that community gardens frequently foster. It reads,

> Our vision is that community gardening is a resource used to build community, foster social and environmental justice, eliminate hunger, empower communities, break down racial and ethnic barriers, provide adequate health and nutrition, reduce crime, improve housing, promote and enhance education, and otherwise create sustainable communities.[6]

Whereas goals like nutrition, eliminating hunger and enhancing education resonate with the stated goals of most community gardens historically, goals such as environmental justice, breaking down ethnic barriers and creating sustainable communities spring from more current cultural trends. These goals do raise the deeper question, though, as to whether a community garden is a good in and of itself or if the good of a community garden is as an instrument or a vehicle for other goods (such as the ones listed above). Hopefully, the three case studies rendered here will help the reader both to reflect more deeply on that question and to reach some conclusions about it.

---

6. Jeanette Abi-Nader, Kendall Dunnigan, and Kristen Markely, *Growing Communities Curriculum* (Philadelphia: American Community Gardening Association, 2001), cited in Lawson, *City Bountiful,* 239.

CHAPTER ONE

Churches, Christ-Centered Community Gardening and Radical Hospitality

I.

ALL OF THIS DISCOURSE about the benefits of gardening and community gardening, though, does not answer the question as to why specifically so many *churches* have decided to launch community gardens. Is it merely a fad? Is it simply that the church is slow to catch up with cultural shifts and so is just now catching on to a trend in community gardening that found its feet back in the 1970s? Is it a trend that will die out as soon as social crises simmer down and the U.S. economy surges forward? Or is the church's increasing openness to the possibility of community gardening as ministry a way of reconnecting with the agricultural practices and worldviews that are deeply embedded in the story of Israel? Can we interpret community gardening as a means of grace, a peculiar way of experiencing creation as sacrament? Who, exactly, constitutes the *community* of community gardening? What *kind* of community does a community garden seek to foster? And what role might a church-sponsored community garden play in mediating the relationship between a local church and her most proximate neighbors?

In the seventeenth century, the (anti)colonialist dissenter Roger Williams once wrote about the vital and lasting need for "a wall of separation between the Garden of Christ and the Wilderness of the World."[1] Of course, for Williams the metaphor of the *Garden of Christ* refers to the Church while the *Wilderness of the World* refers to the civil authority, namely, the state. Williams's invocation of the need for a wall of separation between the church and the state sought to protect the church from interference and harassment by the civil authority's violent policies of enforced conformity. This language of a wall of separation between the church and the state was later adopted by Thomas Jefferson and has influenced the history of the governance of the United States of America in a foundational and lasting way.

Although perhaps this *wall of separation* is an appropriate trope for the relationship between the church and the state, it is obviously *not* a model for the relationship between a church and its most immediate geographical neighbors. Yet, too often in churches today there is a de facto wall of separation between the church and nearby residents to the extent that the church is comprised of very few of them. Instead, in certain contexts increasingly the vast majority of people who show up on Sunday morning for worship commute in from somewhere else. This happens regularly, for example, to churches in established neighborhoods (particularly in historically white neighborhoods) that undergo transition. Even when these church members move out of the neighborhood (the phenomenon known as *white flight*), they will sometimes still return on Sundays for worship. This practice of commuting in for worship also prevails in contexts of suburban sprawl and necessarily with the recent rise of the mega-church. Obviously, when a church hosts fifteen-thousand people for worship on a Sunday morning, the vast majority of these attendees will be commuting in from other neighborhoods, other parts of the city, and indeed from other cities.

1. *Mr. Cotton's Letter Lately Printed, Examined and Answered* 1644

Not surprisingly, with the rise of people commuting in for worship from outside of the immediate environs, the trend for many local churches has involved an increasing estrangement from their closest geographical neighbors. It is important to note that this trend has increased *despite* the fact that most churches would genuinely claim to be open to receiving guests who live nearby. This genuine openness typically takes the form of programs that happen within the church building that may be advertised with signage out front, through advertisements in the newspaper, etc. Yet, despite this openness, churches are frequently left scratching their heads and wondering why nearby residents are not very interested in showing up to the programming that the church is offering.

A fundamental premise of this project is that in order to deconstruct the walls of separation that have formed between many of our local churches and their immediate neighbors, churches must consider engaging nearby residents in concrete ways *outside of the church building* so that the church can actually become a *neighbor* to its neighbors. How might churches effectively welcome nearby residents into new relationships and friendships? What might this form of engagement look like? If this engagement is going to take place outside of the church building, what is it going to look like? How can the church do a better job of meeting people *where they are* (both literally in time and space *and* spiritually)? How can the church discern both the assets of their nearest neighbors (and seek to learn from them) while also discerning the greatest needs of those same neighbors (and seek to serve them)?

As Christians have wrestled with these and similar kinds of questions over the past decade, the number of church-sponsored community gardens in the United States has increased dramatically.[2] Primarily, these community gardens are creations of a local church (sometimes in partnership with another institutional entity) either on or near the church property in which nearby

---

2. Dr. Laura Lawson reported in an email to me that she will be releasing data soon that quantifies this growth in church-sponsored community gardens over the previous decade.

residents are invited to participate. Not surprisingly, the working hypothesis of this project is that church-sponsored and Christ-centered community gardens can help to provide answers to the important questions listed above. Indeed, a core contention of this project is that increasingly church-sponsored community gardens are serving as vehicles for churches to do the kind of outreach that is needed to connect with and to serve those who neighbor their church buildings. These gardens are well-positioned to help churches to meet and to serve their neighbors in novel ways by doing ministry outside of the walls of the church building.

In short, church-sponsored community gardens are proving to be fertile ground not only for the growth of fruits and vegetables, but for the extension of *koinonia* and the cultivation of *neighborhood* among those who inhabit proximate space but who are relationally distant from one another. Since *koinonia* is a gift that the church receives from God, the related concept of cultivating *neighborhood* here names the ways in which the church seeks to extend that gift by sharing it and tending it with others through community gardening. By *neighborhood*, I am invoking the parable of the Good Samaritan and a hope for the creation of a network of relationships characterized not by disinterested and anonymous strangers who live near one another yet "bowl alone." Rather, *neighborhood* consists of persons who both encounter one another in a particular place regularly and whose habits of interaction are characterized by practices of looking one another in the eye and attending to each other in Christ-like ways. In essence, *neighborhood* names a pattern of possibilities of seeing and interacting with others that shifts one's view of them from that of *nearby resident* or *anonymous stranger* to that of *neighbor* (i.e., one who has a claim on my time, my concern and my talents).

Along with the kinds of outreach and missional goals stated above, church-sponsored gardens are serving therapeutic and didactic goals as well. The kinds of therapeutic goals that these gardens serve were elaborated above, namely, the different ways in which gardens foster relaxation, soul restoration and recreation. The didactic goals of church-sponsored community gardens are similarly numerous. First, gardens can serve as a teaching tool that will help the Scriptures to come alive. Since the Israelites were an agricultural people, agricultural themes and metaphors pervade the Bible. Experience with gardening, therefore, deepens and energizes one's understanding of stories such as the parable of the sower, the parable of the tares, the parable of the mustard seed and Jesus' teachings about the harvest. When, for example, one is faced with the arduous task of trying to harvest by one's self a garden full of cherry tomato plants (each plant producing hundreds of cherry tomatoes), Jesus' teaching about *the harvest being plentiful but the laborers being few* (Matthew 9:37) is understood viscerally, not just intellectually.

Just as community gardening can serve as a teaching tool for grounding one's study of the Bible, it can also serve to teach participants about creation care, stewardship and the importance of local food economies. Perhaps part of the social crisis that recent iterations of community gardening address involves the way in which increasingly people are concerned about the national obesity epidemic and the estrangement between people and their sources of food. As people over the past decade have learned more about the dangers of synthetic inputs, nitrogen run-off, pollution and synthetic pesticides, the organic movement has gained both momentum and market shares. Organic gardening, therefore, proves to be one way in which people can learn both how to care for the land and the satisfaction of growing one's own food in sustainable ways. Churches should teach that such practices of sustainability are manifestations of a faithful desire to be careful stewards (borrowers and caretakers) of the gift of land with which the Lord has blessed us. The hope is that in giving to the next generation land and waterways that are less polluted than what we received, we are blessing them, teaching them good manners involving how to borrow and return well, and honoring the Giver of every good gift.

II.

Given that each church must pray and discern what their own strategies of engagement and teaching are going to be, the constructive proposal that this essay calls for and seeks to abet is for churches and church-sponsored institutions to consider launching not just community gardens, but *Christ-centered* community gardens. I first encountered the phrase "Christ-centered community garden" at a workshop at the Christian Community Development Association's National Conference in Indianapolis, IN in October, 2011. I am indebted to the co-leaders of this workshop, Ben Lowe and Steve Fortenberry, for introducing me to the concept. Although I do not recall seeing a specific definition of Christ-centered community gardening proffered during that workshop, the sense conveyed was that such a garden would intentionally have as a part of its purpose, its mission and its norms an *explicit* connection with the way of Christ.

One of the people I talked to during this workshop was a man who serves as the garden director of an established church-sponsored community garden in the southeastern United States. He shared his thoughts with me that a "Christ-centeredness" was what was missing from his garden. He described how easy it is for a "successful" church-sponsored community garden to get caught up in issues of funding, grants and management over the years and to lose whatever initial impulse there may have been of connecting their work with the way of Christ or with a greater mindfulness of the spirituality of gardening. He looked forward to returning from the conference and seeking to instill a greater sense of Christ-centeredness to the workings of the community garden he manages.

For various reasons a church-sponsored community garden may or may not choose to name, articulate and teach how their community garden connects to the way of Christ. It is similarly conceivable that a church-sponsored community garden may have launched with specific intentions to connect its existence and functioning with the way of Christ, but over time that intention may have been forgotten. Given that many community gardens suffer from significant rates of turnover among their participants, how might a Christ-centered community garden remember its founding purpose? What practices, norms or events might help such a garden to stay connected with the way of Christ? And what, after all, does it mean *specifically* to connect the purpose, mission and the norms of a community garden with the way of Christ?

Although many possibilities emerge and different Christian traditions would likely pursue different ways of connecting the mission of their garden with the way of Christ, the constructive connection proposed here involves an emphasis on a radical hospitality that is rooted in the deep welcome of the Lord as witnessed in Jesus Christ. With Christ-centered community gardens, gospel hospitality is a deep welcome that is *intentionally* articulated regularly, practiced through embodied gestures of invitation and friendship, and infused with the kind of virtues associated with the fruit of the Holy Spirit. It is this kind of emphasis that distinguishes Christ-centered community gardening from what is typically called community gardening (church-sponsored or otherwise).

I will spend the remainder of this chapter tracing out contours of what it might mean for a garden to be a space of radical hospitality. First, I will offer some definitions of gospel hospitality. Secondly, I will gesture towards a conception of what might make the kind of hospitality that characterizes Christ-centered community gardens *radical*. Then, we will explore both the traditions and practices of hospitality that emerge in the Bible and throughout the history of the people of God. Ultimately, the hope is that Christ-centered community gardens will cultivate neighborhood by providing space for both church members and nearby residents to experience *radical hospitality* in vibrant and life-giving ways.

In order to flesh out what is meant by gospel hospitality, we will first turn to Amy Oden's book *God's Welcome: Hospitality for a Gospel-Hungry World*. The fundamental definition of gospel hospitality, according to Oden, follows: "Gospel hospitality is God's welcome, a welcome that is deep and wide."[3] Thus, when one talks

3. Amy G. Oden, *God's Welcome: Hospitality For a Gospel-Hungry World* (Cleveland, Ohio: Pilgrim Press, 2008), 11.

about gospel hospitality as a kind of culture or as a practice that grounds an entity like a community garden, the phrase always points first to the welcome that is God's – a welcome that has been made most visible and tangible through the person of Jesus of Nazareth. One discovers the depth and the width of God's welcome in the Bible, for example, in 2 Peter 3:9, "The Lord is not slow about his promise, as some think of slowness, but is patient with you, not wanting any to perish, but all to come to repentance." Thus, God's welcome, God's invitation to us to draw near, to change one's mind about who is Lord and to change the direction of one's life towards God, is an invitation for all, not for a select few. Indeed, it is an invitation for all of creation to participate in the in-breaking Kingdom of God, God's making of all things new.

Before unpacking what a *radical hospitality* might look like, we will first explore other definitions of the term *hospitality* itself. Amy Oden has helpfully culled a list of short definitions from recent scholarship. Hospitality has been defined most basically as "welcoming of the stranger."[4] Reminding us of the term's origins, Hershberger states that hospitality "[in Greek] literally means 'love of stranger.'"[5] According to Pohl, hospitality "is welcoming strangers into a home and offering them food, shelter, and protection."[6] Defining the term more broadly, Nouwen claims that hospitality "is a fundamental attitude toward our fellow human being."[7] Similarly, Koenig affirms that it "is also a matter of human exchanges that restore the spirit."[8] This final definition from Koenig points

---

4. Amy G. Oden, ed., *And You Welcomed Me: a Sourcebook On Hospitality in Early Christianity* (Nashville: Abingdon Press, 2001), 13.

5. Michele Hershberger, *A Christian View of Hospitality: Expecting Surprises* (Scottdale, Pa.: Herald Pr, 1999), 20.

6. Christine D. Pohl, *Making Room: Recovering Hospitality as a Christian Tradition* (Grand Rapids, Mich.: William B. Eerdmans Publishing Company, 1999), 4.

7. Henri J.M. Nouwen, *Reaching Out: the Three Movements of the Spiritual Life* (Garden City, N.Y.: Image, 1986), 67.

8. John Koenig, *New Testament Hospitality: Partnership with Strangers as Promise and Mission* (Eugene, OR: Wipf & Stock Publishers, 2001), 1.

to the reciprocity and mutuality that is latent in all of the above definitions and inherent in the practice of hospitality.

Expanding on that primary definition, Oden connects God's welcome with an invitation to participate in the life of God. She writes, "Gospel hospitality is God's welcome into a new way of seeing and living. Ultimately, gospel hospitality is God's welcome into abundant life, into God's own life."[9] So what is this "new way of seeing and living"? It involves a way of seeing the stranger not as someone to fear and to distrust, but as someone who comes as a bearer of the divine image. It includes opening up the sacred spaces of our lives and inviting other people in. It requires a patience and an openness to sharing our time, our attention, our love, our talents and our treasures with the person God places before us.

But what exactly differentiates *gospel* hospitality from more common constructions of hospitality? One might assert that since gospel hospitality is God's welcome, to the extent that our hospitality of others is a sharing in God's welcoming of us it should be marked by the fruit of the Holy Spirit. Another way of approaching that question would be to search out correspondences and discrepancies between the ways a church-sponsored community garden, for example, practices hospitality and the examples of hospitality that we discover in the Bible. Oden affirms, "Scripture is packed with stories of hospitality, stories of God's own welcome sometimes through a host, often through a guest or stranger, a welcome that is often full of surprises, for both host and guest."[10] One thinks of Abraham and Sarah's welcoming of the three visitors in Genesis 18, or of the welcome the travelers to Emmaus offered to the stranger on the road in Luke 24. According to Oden, what is crucial in these stories is the way in which *both* guest and host are changed in these stories because of the hospitality that was extended.

One of the beautiful things about church-sponsored community gardening is that the community of gardeners that forms there has both physical and spiritual food to share with one another and

9. Oden, *God's Welcome*, 11.

10. Ibid.

with hungry neighbors. Without a doubt, there are people drawn to church-sponsored community gardens who suffer from food insecurity. Similarly, there are others who are involved with these gardens who, although their bellies are full, are yet hungry for a deeper experience of life and God. As Oden attests:

> Spiritual wanderers – those spiritually starved and denied – show up at our doors, not because they like our buildings or even because they like us, but because they are hungry. Hungry for forgiveness, for rest and peace. Hungry for mercy and grace. Hungry to explore and grow. Hungry for the good news of new life, of abundant life. Hungry for God to do a new thing.[11]

Although Oden is not referring explicitly to church-sponsored community gardens here as the event or the space to which hungry people show up, since these gardens function as an extension of the ministry of the church they fit with the description she offers. To put it tersely, one might say that the kind of culture that a Christ-centered community garden seeks to make is one in which the hungry are fed both physically and spiritually.

Admittedly, although it is easy to see the ways in which a Christ-centered community garden feeds the physical needs of those involved, it is less simple to name the specific ways in which the garden feeds one spiritually. Different people would undoubtedly name different spiritual blessings through their involvement with a church-sponsored community garden; conceivably these could include the therapeutic benefits of putting one's hands in the soil and participating in the creation of plant life, connecting with other gardeners through shared labor and conversations, growing more attuned to the seasons and developing an increased sense of the sacramentality of creation, learning to pray for rain, or (as mentioned earlier) experiencing the many parables and teachings of Christ that have to do with farming come alive in a new way. Oden confirms that, "The point of gospel hospitality is to invite others to experience the living, welcoming God and to experience

---

11. Ibid, 12.

the living, welcoming God in others."[12] Our first case study, Anathoth Community Garden, serves as an example of this kind of invitation; it was created as a space where the interaction between strangers is intended to foster reconciliation. As the reader will discover shortly, Anathoth serves as a vehicle that helps participants to experience a culture of gospel hospitality in which to "experience the living, welcoming God in others."

But in order to extend and to experience this kind of hospitality in a church-sponsored community garden, it requires work; it requires concrete practices of mindfulness, of paying attention. Commenting on the *spirituality* of gospel hospitality as it is lived out in the real world, Oden declares:

> How do we live gospel hospitality in real life? Throughout the centuries, Christians have called the intentional and mindful living out of our faith "spirituality." Spirituality can sound fluffy or insubstantial, but in truth it is made up of concrete, everyday *practices* that pay attention to God. A spirituality of hospitality is the particular practice of *paying attention to God's welcome* in our lives and paying attention to the welcome we extend to others.[13]

Given this definition, one discerns the importance of paying attention to the spirituality of gospel hospitality. But, one might fairly ask, when Oden directs her readers to "concrete, everyday practices that pay attention to God" and "to God's welcome in our lives," to what specifically is she pointing? Although she offers no exhaustive list, one can assume she is describing, for example, concrete practices such as prayer, journaling, Bible study, serving at a food bank, volunteering at a hospital, and taking your sick neighbor some chicken noodle soup. Certainly, Christ-centered community gardening could be included in a list such as this to the extent that the digging, the planting, the pulling weeds, the camaraderie of two people working to pull a U-bar down to break up some earth, the paying attention to the particular details of soil, soil acidity, weather, season, seed, seed depth, space between

12. Ibid, 15.

13. Ibid, 53.

seeds, crop rotation and crop fertilization, for example, helps to engender the kind of mindfulness of God to which Oden points.

Such mindfulness, in turn, forms the gardener into the kind of person who can pay attention to the ways in which God has welcomed us. Here one might question, "welcomed us" into what, specifically? One could answer this question in a number of ways, but perhaps the primary answer would be that God has invited all of creation to experience the restoration and renewal of participating in the triune life of God. Speaking to this issue about the ways in which practices of hospitality form practitioners in fruitful ways, Oden states:

> The purpose of the concrete practices of Christian spirituality and, in this case, practices that develop a mindfulness of God's welcome, is to shape our hearts as well as our action. God's welcome starts to become who we are, not just what we do. Paying attention helps us embody hospitality deep in our bones. By paying attention, we not only live in welcome. Gospel hospitality lives in us.[14]

Thus, for Oden, concrete practices of spirituality engender a transformation by which hospitality names not so much what we do, but who we are; that the entirety of our lives becomes an extension of the divine welcome that we have received and that inhabits us increasingly.

Even though all of the definitions above will lurk connotatively, a combination of a few of these definitions will provide the operative definition of hospitality that underwrites this project. Thus, hospitality names *those restorative exchanges between strangers that embody and enact our welcome into the life of God*. But what exactly makes this kind of hospitality *radical*? By radical, I am not referring primarily to the connotations of the word that have to do with the extreme. Rather, I am pointing towards the term's etymology which has to do with the notion of "root." Therefore, a *radical hospitality* would involve *restorative exchanges of welcome that are deeply rooted to a particular place, a specific piece*

14. Ibid, 53–4.

of land that provides creative, liminal and disruptive space for the performance of God's welcome.

Having established working definitions of gospel hospitality and radical hospitality, we will turn towards Christine Pohl's book *Making Room: Recovering Hospitality as a Christian Tradition* in order both to flesh out connotations and to name implications for a thick practice of radical hospitality that is rooted in the traditions of Christianity and that could ground the purpose, mission and goals of Christ-centered community gardening. How does, for example, the traditional conception of hospitality relate to contemporary understandings of the term in North American popular culture? Pohl asserts:

> Although we often think of hospitality as a tame and pleasant practice, Christian hospitality has always had a subversive, countercultural dimension. "Hospitality is resistance," as one person from the Catholic Worker observed. Especially when the larger society disregards or dishonors certain persons, small acts of respect and welcome are potent far beyond themselves. They point to a different system of valuing and an alternate model of relationships.[15]

Thus, hospitality in the Christian tradition is not concerned with the quotidian specifics of middle-class customs of welcoming a guest; nor is it concerned with merely decorative or superficial matters, for example. Instead, the tradition of Christian hospitality points towards "a different system of valuing and an alternate model of relationships" that might best be summed up as the inbreaking Kingdom of God and the gathered *ekklesia* charged with witnessing holistically to its reality.

According to Pohl, an important part of this "different system" and "alternative model" involves the capacity to *recognize* the stranger as one who is worthy of one's time, love and concern. But what is the basis of this kind of recognition? To answer that question, Pohl turns to John Calvin who has, in Pohl's estimation,

15. Pohl, *Making Room*, 61. Pohl's citation for the embedded quotation reads: Bernard Connaughton, *Catholic Worker*, June/July 1996, p.2.

"developed one of the most comprehensive foundations for a generous response to strangers".[16] Because in this quotation Calvin helpfully answered potential objections to the Christian's duty to recognize the stranger with generous receptivity, it is worth quoting in full:

> Therefore, whatever man you meet who needs your aid, you have no reason to refuse to help him. Say, "He is a stranger"; but the Lord has given him a mark that ought to be familiar to you, by virtue of the fact that he forbids you to despise your own flesh (Isa. 58:7, Vg). Say, "He is contemptible and worthless"; but the Lord shows him to be one to whom he has deigned to give the beauty of his image. Say that you owe nothing for any service of his; but God, as it were, has put him in his own place in order that you may recognize toward him the many and great benefits with which God has bound you to himself. Say that he does not deserve even your least effort for his sake; but the image of God, which recommends him to you, is worthy of your giving yourself and all your possessions.[17]

Thus, for Calvin, because of the *imago dei* there is no valid excuse for Christians to ignore the one who might need our aid. Certainly, were such hospitality to be practiced regularly by churches, this practice would both disrupt the normal routines of church members and risk the accomplishment of other goals that those members or that church may have set for themselves. Indeed, such practice would embody "resistance" against broader cultural assumptions about what is important and who is worth spending time with.

Later, Pohl highlights John Chrysostom's crucial reminder that within the Christian practice of hospitality, it is not just one's actions but one's intentions and disposition-while-welcoming that matter greatly. Pohl explains, "Chrysostom stressed the importance of respect and humility in offering hospitality, criticizing

16. Ibid, 64.

17. Calvin, *Institutes of the Christian Religion*, 2 vols., ed. John T. McNeill (Philadelphia: Westminster Press, 1960), 3.7.6. Cited in Pohl, 64.

those who 'think themselves superior to the recipients, and often-times despise them for the attention given to them.'"[18] Chrysostom here points to the importance of the *posture* that Christians adopt as we welcome strangers into our midst. As we *serve*, we must also exercise the openness, curiosity and expectation of God showing up that will enable us to *learn* from God and from those we serve. As Pohl elaborates, "Here Chrysostom identifies a particularly difficult problem in ministry: that practitioners, while offering a service, can come to disrespect those who receive it, simply be-cause of their weakness and need."[19] Sadly, if one is not serving with humility and grace, her attempts to help may actually harm the recipients by belittling their dignity. Such attempts could also hurt the one doing the "helping" by reinforcing hubris, arrogance and a "thank God I'm not like that person" disposition.

However, when hospitality is offered by church members with a spirit of humility and grace, their welcome of strangers extends the gracious welcome of God and points eschatologically to the hope that motivates the Church. "In some churches," Pohl contends, "expanding the hospitality that members offer to one another would be an important first step."[20] Such a step might seem obvious, but given the history of many white churches in the United States, for example, and their complicity with policies of segregation and exclusion, the need to teach the Church's respon-sibility for extending welcome to the stranger exists. As Pohl in-forms, "Occasionally, churches embrace a model of hospitality to strangers in an attempt *to get past* racial, ethnic, and other distinc-tions. A gracious spirit of welcome, equality, and care can help in efforts to heal racial divisions and previous exclusions. Generous

18. Pohl, *Making Room*, 69. Pohl's citation for the embedded quotation reads: Chrysostom, Homily 41 on Genesis, in Homilies on Genesis 18–45, trans. Robert C. Hill, The Fathers of the Church, vol. 82 (Washington D.C.: Catholic University of America Press, 1990), 413.

19. Pohl, *Making Room*, 69–70.

20. Ibid, 157.

and steady hospitality, practiced among believers from different backgrounds can be the beginning of significant reconciliation."[21]

Indeed, the kind of "generous and steady" hospitality that would norm the operation of a Christ-centered community garden would be one in which small but significant gestures of reconciliation could regularly take place. For example, perhaps church members who quarrel in business meetings could find common ground by talking their differences out as they spread compost together. Perhaps church members who own homes in nearby suburbs could build relationships with nearby residents who live in apartment buildings and have no access to land by planting onions together. Perhaps Republican and Democratic church members could offer hospitality to *the stranger within* through actually listening to one another and achieving charitable disagreements even in an election year while pulling weeds together, etc.

Although a church probably should offer some of the produce from its Christ-centered community garden to nearby residents in need, the descriptions of relationship-building described above remind us that sometimes the Church does a much better job of handing out food than it does of extending itself and its relationships in life-giving ways. Pohl affirms, "Congregations

21. Ibid. Italics mine. This language of "getting past" difference marks an important place of disagreement between Pohl and myself. This kind of language is also present in Pohl's earlier question on p.64, "What theological understandings help Christians *to transcend* difference, resist indifference, and welcome inconvenient strangers?" (italics mine). Although I am deeply sympathetic to the overall goal of Pohl's intentions here (which I take to be preventing difference from being a barrier to providing love and welcome), her language of *getting past* and *transcending* difference assumes that the Christian cannot learn to love the concrete otherness of the other, but instead must transcend that difference, must get beyond and escape that concrete otherness, in order to learn to love them. Her argument would be further strengthened if instead of using the language of *transcending* difference, she were use the language of *embracing* difference, *embracing* the concrete otherness of the other; looking embodied alterity in the eye and saying, "Welcome." This kind of embrace was modeled in the Incarnation, after all, in which the Trinitarian welcome was extended to humanity not by the Son's *transcending* human flesh (that ultimate concrete otherness of the created other), but by *embracing* human flesh, inhabiting it, and dwelling among us.

committed to ministering to people in need sometimes overlook their own greatest resource – the fellowship of believers."[22] Pohl continues by describing Kathryn Mowry's articulation of the distinction between "church" and "mission." The basic idea is that the church becomes limited to those inside the church walls while the mission entails the serving of needy others that happens outside of the church's worship and fellowship times (and typically outside of the church walls).[23] "Churches have generally done better," Pohl concludes, "with offering food programs and clothing closets than with welcoming into worship people significantly different from their congregations."[24]

Without a doubt, difference is difficult to embrace. It is much easier to provide charity towards those who are different than it is to open ourselves up to the transformational power of God experienced through sharing life together with those who are different. Encountering difference with humility, grace, curiosity and openness is not easy, but a core presupposition of this project is that it becomes easier when persons are actually *doing* activities together. An important part of the great potential of Christ-centered community gardening involves the ways in which the practices of gardening when done with others (indeed there are things that need to be done in a garden that can *only* be done with the help of others) lend themselves to conversation, to asking for and offering help, to teaching and learning, to intergenerational interaction,[25] and to the proven therapeutic benefits of getting one's hands in the dirt. Indeed, as Christ-centered community garden participants (church members and nearby neighbors of the garden) harvest

22. Pohl, *Making Room*, 159.

23. See Kathryn Mowry, "Do Good Fences Make Good Neighbors?" in God So Loves the City, ed. Charles Van Engen and Jude Tiersma (World Vision: MARC, 1994), 117. Cited in Pohl, *Making Room*, 159.

24. Pohl, *Making Room*, 160.

25. As ministries in the church continue to become increasingly segregated according to age demographics, Christ-centered community gardening proves to be an effective vehicle for intergenerational ministry as young people and novice gardeners learn from the adults and older adults who have years of gardening experience.

peppers together and learn one another's names, as they water tender plants in the heat of July together and build relationships with one another, as they laugh together and sweat together and pray together on that good soil, as radical hospitality is offered to the strangers who show up to garden, the rigid distinction between church and mission is destabilized and a new neighborhood is cultivated.

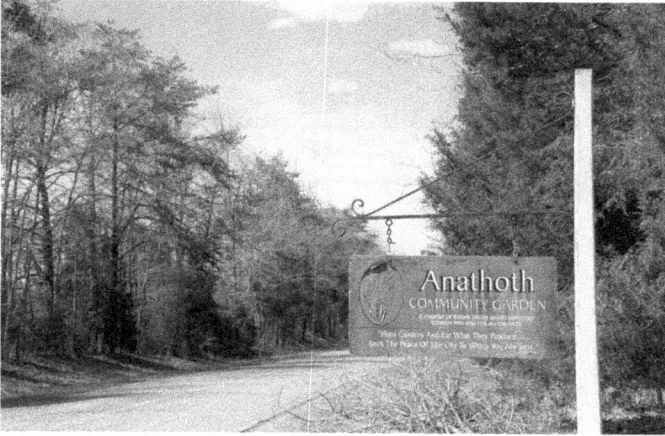

This sign greets you as you enter Anathoth Community Garden in Cedar Grove, N.C. The biblical quotation on the bottom of the sign comes from Jeremiah 29:5 and 7. Photographer: Adam Standiford

Although it is difficult to make out from this photo, the beds being worked in the background of this photograph are in the shape of a Celtic cross. In the foreground are rows of strawberries. Photographer: Adam Standiford

The hoophouse in the background helps to extend the growing
season. Notice also the chicken coop to the left.
Photographer: Adam Standiford

The extraordinary raised bed in the middle-right of the picture was
created to allow folks in wheelchairs or with back issues to be able to
garden at Anathoth. Photographer: Adam Standiford

CHAPTER TWO

Cultivating Healing

*An Interview with Rev. Grace Hackney on the
Origins of Anathoth Community Garden in
Cedar Grove, North Carolina*

First Case Study

Interview Date: 3/15/11

ANATHOTH IS A CHURCH-SPONSORED community garden in
Cedar Grove, N.C. that was launched in 2004. This garden is
distinctive in that its birth stems directly from a very specific in-
stance of social crisis in the small country crossroads called Cedar Grove, namely, the execution-style murder of a shopkeeper
in his bait and tackle store. Anathoth Community Garden, then,
was born out of the community's response to this terrible trag-
edy, this social crisis. As such, one could narrate Anathoth's birth
as an intentional act of *culture making* (to borrow Andy Crouch's
phrase). But, one might appropriately ask, specifically what *kind*
of culture is Anathoth thereby producing? As the case-study of

Anathoth will make clear, the hope is that the kind of culture being produced at Anathoth is one marked by a radical hospitality in which the reconciliation of old divisions takes root and violence does not happen. Indeed, Crouch's conception of culture making and the theme of gospel hospitality can help to inform constructively the purposes and the goals of church-sponsored community gardening.

Interview with Rev. Grace Hackney

Bryan: *Grace, maybe if you could just begin by sharing a little bit about the origins of how the community garden called Anathoth was started, the backstory of the whole thing.*

Grace: Sure. We had, it was at the time of the tobacco buy-outs in North Carolina. And myself and a few other people had been really concerned about the use of land in Cedar Grove. And also about that same time NPR did a talk on poverty, a series on poverty in North Carolina. And so all of these little pieces sort of started coming together and we learned that the new look of poverty in North Carolina was obesity. And also that seventy percent of people that live in poverty live in rural areas. And so putting those things together, it just seemed, you know, sinful that there would be in rural areas, those places where there is plenty of land but people are not eating well. Instead they're eating you know the high calorie, low cost food.

And so we started having these conversations that we called Food, Farm and Faith; we'd just talk about those issues and we opened it up to anybody that wanted to come…We probably only had four or five, but we invited whoever wanted to come and a couple of tobacco farmers came. And so other people from the church and just other interested people, not a ton of folks came. But we just sort of started studying that issue and kind of looking at it theologically as a church. What did it mean that we had this gift of land all around us? And then at the same time we're building the new church that had been burned down by fire and we entered into the book of Jeremiah. And so that further challenged us and you know Jeremiah is called to build and plant, you know, was one of the things. And then here we are building this new church and sometimes we look at that very metaphorically, but we started thinking about what it would be if we didn't look at it metaphorically. What if we started really looking at that literally?

And it was about that time that there was the murder, and as a matter of fact the murder was at the beginning of the summer in 2004. And it just brought up another issue in the community and that was that of racial reconciliation. And we started thinking that the reconciliation of the land and the reconciliation of races and reconciliation in general was one subject; it was one topic and not separate topics – that there was this connection. By the way and I haven't often told this part of the story but I also learned that the Alex Haley story of *Roots* kind of took place in that part of North Carolina; that was some of the origins of Alex Haley's story *Roots*. So that was sort of in the background.

After the murder of Bill King, we had had conversations a little bit with Valee Taylor at the post office. I just introduced myself to him and told him that if he needed anything to let us know. He had come and asked if we could help with a fundraiser to find the murderer. But after we talked for a while we realized that maybe a better thing to do would be to do a prayer vigil because there had been no memorial service or anything for Bill King. And so on the two week anniversary we did this prayer vigil there at the store and it was probably, from what people tell me because I was still a newcomer in the community, it was probably one of the first times that the races had come together.

Bryan: *Was Bill King an African-American?*

Grace: He was white and his wife was black, his common-law wife was black. And they had African-American children through her first husband. And he [Bill King] was a poor store owner but well-respected in the community. He had kind of cleaned up that corner there. The previous store owner had… there had been a lot of drug trade, etc., and it was a really unsafe part of Cedar Grove. And so he had come in and just wouldn't take that anymore and you know, let people have food on loan.

So when he was murdered and we did the prayer vigil, Scenobia Taylor just felt that, she felt a connection with me and she had had this vision that she wanted to give land to someone in the community that would use it for reconciliation in the community, that would use it for the community. And so she asked Fred [Bahnson] and I to come and talk to her about what we thought would be a good way to do that. And she had had this vision as well of some kind of a garden and so her vision and our vision kind of came together, which was pretty amazing. That's the short part of the story. Did you see the [Duke] Divinity [School] magazine last Fall that had the article in it?

Bryan: *I did, I'm pretty sure . . . I don't recall specifics but I'm sure I did.*

Grace: I think it was called "Abundance at Anathoth." That tells a little bit more of the story from their perspective.

Bryan: *From the Taylor's?*

Grace: Yes.

Bryan: *And you mentioned Fred, who is Fred?*

Grace: Fred Bahnson was actually a preceptor at the Div [Duke Divinity] School and Elizabeth was his wife who was my field ed[ucation] student. Elizabeth was part of the Food/Faith conversations that we had early on, but she was there as my field ed student when the murder happened. And so it's just like all of these little pieces started coming together. Fred had always wanted his theology to be grounded in a more practical, agrarian kind of way and at that time that was a new thought. I mean really in 2004 we weren't seeing a lot of faith-based community gardens, etc. So it was kind of a radical, [laughter] a radical thought.

Bryan: *Sure. So how did it go from that idea...describe for me the early stages of implementing it. So you were given this land...*

Grace: Well she wanted to offer us five acres of land which Jeff Gledhill, who is a lawyer and a member of our church offered to give his time as a lawyer to help us to figure out what was the best way to do that. We went to the church council. They were, um, skeptical, at best. I mean I think the big question was, why would a church want to have a garden? And under that was, if we are going to have a garden why would we want to have it down there? Why not...there were plenty of people in the church that had other land.

And so to be quite honest we went through a couple of different council meetings, and because Duke Endowment had already sort of gotten on board and said, "wow, this is something we would want to fund" even before we wrote a grant because I had talked to Joe Mann about this vision, etc. Because the church wasn't going to have to take a financial [hit], I think it was sort of like, "Yeah go ahead and start your little garden, and you know in a year or two you'll get tired of it." And so really I think the Council approved it pretty easily because they didn't think it was going to happen. Or, not everybody, I shouldn't say that. There were certainly people who were in on the vision and saw the potential. But there were others who were a little bit more the naysayers who were just like, "Yeah, have your fun for a little bit. You're going to find out how hard farming is, and it's not going to work."

So after the Council approved it and we wrote the grant to Duke Endowment, I mean everything happened really quickly. It was just, we hired Fred...Fred actually started working for free because even though the grant wasn't going to get approved until effective December of that year – that would have been 2005, we felt pretty confident that we were going to go forward with it. And so he started working before we actually got the money. And we also learned that there was a need for places for youth to work out their volunteer community service hours in the county. There were a lot of places in town, but there wasn't much in the county. And so we made this connection with Volunteers for Youth.

So in some ways I think we kind of went around it the back door, and sort of went out to prove ourselves, rather than doing it the other way around and saying we're going to build our case and then get approval. And I'm not sure one way's better than another. But as I've thought about it, I've thought we sort of went out on a limb, trusting. And I think the people that were in on the ground, we just knew that this was a vision from God and that it, and that all the pieces were falling together in such amazing ways. Somebody's giving us land, Fred fell into our lap that had this dream and this desire. Duke Endowment is wanting to do this kind of thing where there is community collaboration. I mean it just, everything fell into place. The Volunteers for Youth thing fell into place. We had several different groups that heard about it who wanted to donate money up front, like Bruederhoff – I don't know if you're familiar with them. They donated $5,000 for the greenhouse and brought a group down to help us get started. And so there were just a lot of pieces that kind of just effortlessly fell into place early on.

Bryan: *That's amazing. So then...how did...my understanding is that early on the membership of the garden was about half folks from the church and half folks from the community. How did that...getting folks plugged in, what was that process like?*

Grace: What we did is we tried to develop a board because we had to have a board to do the Duke Endowment; that was part of their requirement. And so the initial Food, Faith and Farming conversations that we had, we let those people know. We thought of people that we would need to be on the board, and Fred and I went, John Hughes (you know John), we went and invited people to be part of this. You know we knew we needed some racial diversity. We knew we needed non-church people. And so we invited people to be part of that and early on we had a number of just sort of very informal daydreaming conversations at the church.

It went through a lot of different morphs of what this might look like. And there were a lot of people that had a lot of energy at the beginning that, they didn't stick with it for one reason or another. But then we had other people that would hear about it and would want to get in on it. And we taught this class, the Just Eating class, and actually had some students from the Div school that came out for that. And Joe Mann started bringing his Rural Church class out and other people started bringing, even before we had a lot happening, people were catching on to just the idea. And so that kind of helped us get going on it.

Plus, I think my preaching changed when all of this started happening because like I said we were in Jeremiah and so all of a sudden I felt like I was reading the Scripture through a different kind of lens, which brought a lot of good but it also brought some conflict. And that's probably something you're going to ask...I'll just jump to it right now is that it was a very different theology than a lot of people...it's not a personal salvation theology. It's a looking at that John 3:16 passage, you know "for God so loved the world," and what we mean by that, and that it's not a personal salvation but that there's this interconnectedness with all of creation. And there were also folks who were concerned that we would be spending money on this while we were still building a church that wasn't paid for, and that Duke Endowment would actually give us more money for this, or as much money for this as they would give for a church building.

Bryan: *Oh...is there any truth to that?*

Grace: We did get money through the Duke Endowment for the church building, but we got continued money for the garden. And I think people were...it was just a new mindset, I mean it's a very new mindset and it's going to make things look different. And the church started looking different, new people started coming to church, and anytime that happens there's just, "What's happening to us?" There's always going to be some, just questioning. And as time went on and folks saw that it was not going to fizzle out, but just the opposite of that…it was flourishing and we were getting attention and people started getting on board. I would say there were a few families who never got on board and who were always thorns in our side. But for the most part we did, we were connected with Caring Communities at Duke and Keith Meador was the leader of that at that time. You remember Keith?

Bryan: *Absolutely.*

Grace: So through Caring Communities we offered a series of conferences. And the first one we did at Cedar Grove…you know we invited people from all over the state and Norman [Wirzba] was our speaker and it was just very well attended. We had some of the older farmers tell their stories about farming and I actually have the dvd's of those.

Bryan: *And that was at the church building?*

Grace: That was at the church building. And so we started getting attention for what we were doing which doesn't always happen now because it's not as uncommon a thing. Plus we had this story about this murder to go with it. So I think our circumstance has been a little different than a lot of circumstances and we had other places start calling us and saying, "How can we do this?" So our initial vision of doing this in the community grew to be this vision where maybe we could be a teaching place where it's not just about growing food and it's not just about reconciliation in our own community but it's about sharing that information.

Bryan: *During those initial conversations and that initial skepticism, was there any intentionality or did there need to be about connecting the purposes of the garden or the goals of the garden with the mission of the church?*

Grace: I think one of the things that helped is that even though…I think in general the church population was excited that this might bring new people to church. Even though you are always going to have your few, but…

Bryan: *It did…*

Grace: It did. Oh yeah, it definitely did. And so seeing that as a mission, and also you know the mission that Jesus says, "Inasmuch as you do to the least of these, you've done this to me." So the whole Matthew 25…so seeing that as a mission of the church to be outside the walls and in the community. A lot of people that I think had sort of been missing that part of the mission of the church really were just charged by it and transformed, transformed by it.

And we started doing an annual blessing of the seeds and soil, kind of a Rogation Day, the old Rogation Day; we started doing that where people brought in things from their farms for us to bless. This year we did that on Creation Care Sunday that's set through the Methodist Calendar and this year that day is on Easter Sunday; kind of interesting. We did our Vacation Bible School around that theme. Again I told you the Just Eating class.

And during the middle of all that also the thing that came up that was challenging was the whole idea of nationalism. It came up in the middle of all of that…just looking at ourselves more as a global kind of community. And in the conversations it just sort of would come up that America's pretty greedy, or as Americans we have this high materialism kind of thing. And setting ourselves apart as Christians and not letting America be our greatest identity but looking at Christians and that was threatening; that was very threatening to folks in the South. So that all happened at about the same…that could have happened whether we had the garden or not I think. But the fact that the garden was happening kind of just exacerbated it some.

Bryan: *So it sounds like it involved teaching, classes, a lot of preaching, to try to help folks make the connection between what the work of the church is and how this garden could be a vehicle for what we're trying to accomplish.*

Grace: Exactly.

Bryan: *Because that's not obvious to many of us or to a lot of people what those connections are.*

Grace: And when that light bulb starts going off, that's then where we would get the energy from people who would volunteer or donate money or talk about it…lots of teaching within the church as well as outside the church. And I think one of the things I've said is that this isn't just a ministry or a program that's going to go away. Instead it's an invitation into a kind of lifestyle. So it's not just a three year ministry we're going to do and evaluate it afterwards. So from the get-go it was articulated as *this is an invitation to a way of life* that's kind of counter from what we are mostly offered. And, you know that as Christians, undoing that dualism again between body and spirit and that our bodies matter. So tons of teaching, tons of teaching and listening and going forward when one hundred percent of the people were not on board.

Bryan: *One of the things when you talk about an invitation to a different lifestyle, I'm struck just with the time that I've spent at Anathoth, it seems like a part of that invitation and a part of that alternative is…in the culture of the United States efficiency and convenience are such…I've tried to watch commercials recently with an eye for how are they marketing efficiency and convenience. It's everywhere and everything. But I see in some of the decisions that were made early on that efficiency and convenience were not going to be driving, motivating things.*

Grace: I think you're right.

Bryan: *So maybe you could speak about some of the early decisions that were made that invite us to an alternative to a lifestyle that is based on efficiency and convenience.*

Grace: Well, when you grow your own food, that takes time…and it takes patience and it kind of invites you in to this different narrative of not doing it as quickly as you can or not trying to produce a desired outcome. Rather, you know we're going to plant these tomatoes and we're going to nurture them and they might not make it [laughs]. And so there is this ingrained, deep trust in God and so God is part of the formula. You know we're going to help out with sprinkling; we're not only going to rely on God giving us the rain. But this…we're not going to look at food as a commodity as far as we're going to buy the cheapest thing we can get or we're going to only get what's on sale or we're going to buy in bulk; you know, the whole manna story…that learning what it means to be grateful and eating what's in season is one way to do that.

But then also using our bodies to do the work and so not having a lot of big equipment to come in and just get it done in a day or two. We made some really, Fred…probably one of the early riffs between older farmers and Fred was that he didn't want to use any tractors. And he kind of swallowed his words a little bit on that one because he did finally say "yeah we've got to have someone come here and bushwhack all this down." But, all the beds were dug by hand. And again that…the discipline of labor, of physical labor that our society has lost. So we made real intentional decisions early on that what we were doing is as important as how we were doing it, but the two couldn't be separated. I don't know if that answers your question.

Bryan: *Absolutely because I was on the U-bar [a large non-mechanized farm instrument for breaking up earth] yesterday and…*

Grace: Are you sore today?

Bryan: *A little bit, yeah…different muscles than I'm used to using. But I'm struck because just in some of the conversations at the church that I'm at, some of the initial conversations about the possibility of doing a garden, one of the things that I kept coming back to that I think I learned at Anathoth that I kept sharing with folks is… folks* *were saying, "Oh, the soil's not good. You won't grow anything out there. There could be vandalism" and all this stuff. The point I kept coming back to is that it's the process that matters more…*

Grace: And we had those same questions and as a matter of fact the whole idea of vandalism came up early on, about needing a gate. And again, looking at that theologically, you know, what's our purpose? Is our purpose to see if we can produce enough food to feed all of Cedar Grove? That was not our purpose. We didn't have a production mode purpose. And that's a temptation, that's a very real temptation…and so what if somebody comes in and takes some of the food? Maybe that person needs it. And interestingly enough we've never had a problem with vandalism. The same thing about, certainly we would have community meetings to talk about what are things we're going to plant this next year, etc., but I don't think we ever had a community meeting that said that we want to produce x amount of pounds of this or whatever. And that whatever was going to be produced, that was going to be enough to share with the community. So maybe we would have fewer tomatoes one year than we would another year, but…

Bryan: *It almost sounds like recreation as opposed to productivity is sort of motivating…because with recreation it's not…*

Grace: More the process.

Bryan: *Right, as opposed to having something at the end to show.*

Grace: And kind of honoring the Sabbath cycle too. We had some interesting questions early on like, "Could you go work on Sunday at the Garden?" And we decided *no*, that we wanted it to lay fallow on Sundays and…if you needed a tomato, then go down and pick yourself a tomato, but let's not be working on Sunday. And I don't know if…and because we were ecumenical and there were people of other faiths working there the question came up and we just sort of decided that "yes we're open to any faith but we are a

Christian community garden so we're going to ask you to honor the Sabbath."

Bryan: *That's neat. I didn't know that.*

Grace: Yeah, and if you wanted to come have a picnic down there on Sunday, sure, come do it. But let's not be weeding the garden or...

Bryan: *Using the u-bar on the Sabbath...*

Grace: Yeah.

Bryan: *What would you say surprised you most just in the first year of the garden? What surprised you most about what happened with it?*

Grace: I undoubtedly, it's just how it all came together. It's like, it just happened. I mean all of the pieces just fell in place, more than we could have imagined. We had this open kind of vision: we're going to do a garden and we're going to grow food, and we'll do it this certain way. But it just far exceeded our expectations. And I think I was also really surprised by just the curiosity factor, that people were like "Oh." You know for me it was like, "Oh, we're going to do a garden." I grew up having a garden. But it was...I think there was a much higher learning curve for a lot of people than I expected.

Bryan: *As far as gardening itself?*

Grace: Uh-huh.

Bryan: *Or that it was a church garden?*

Grace: Both. We got asked a lot of times, "Why would a church have a garden?" To me it just made perfect sense. I was like, "Why not?" The church is the best place to do this work in my mind, but sometimes we take for granted that our assumptions are public generalizations and they're not.

Bryan: *That's true. You know one of the things that really excites me about the possibility of the garden where I'm at is that it seems like ministry, increasingly just from what I've noticed, is divided demographically, by age. And so it seems like a garden is a great place for intergenerational ministry...*

Grace: I think you're right.

Bryan: *And intergenerational work together. And I think that's great. I think we need to try to create space for that. But have you all found that that happens?*

Grace: Definitely. I think that we probably could have been a little more careful at the beginning about some of the attitudes of some of the older farmers. I think there were a generation or a couple of generations of farmers who felt threatened, like you know, "I've done this. I know how to do this. It's hard work. What? You're not going to use any kind of chemicals? How are you going to do that?" And so there was this skepticism and rather than slowing down and involving them in the process, etc., we just went ahead.

And some of those farmers came on board. I mean, they would just come down out of curiosity to see if we're making it or not. And I remember Bill Ray saying, "These are the best...this is amazing, just complimenting us...this is the most beautiful garden I've ever seen. This is amazing." And Dwight Oakley who grows a huge garden every year said, "This is beautiful but I'm going to keep doing it the way I'm doing it." And we're like, "Sure. Keep doing it the way you're doing it." And so trying not to be purists, you know. If it's local, we're going to...we do this food sharing thing in the parking lot at the church before we started getting full harvests where if you had extra food from your garden just bring it and whoever needs it can come and get it. And there got to be this, after the garden got started, there got to be this, even though we didn't say it, there got to be this kind of elitist thing going on like, "Oh, I can't bring my zucchini because I dusted them with something, and my food is inferior to your food." And I think we could've done a better job at that. Fred confesses as well that he was pretty…purist about what we're going to do. But in some ways I think you do need to do, to be that in some ways. So we may have alienated some of the older farmers early on because we didn't use some of their skills.

Bryan: *Some of those decisions that were made early on, being organic, not using farm tools – I mean mechanized, for the most part – and for example not doing individual plots but having it farmed communally, was that the board that made those decisions? Or was that Fred's thing? Or how were those decisions made early on?*

Grace: I think we just…I don't know that we sat down and said "Ok, how are we going to do this?" I think it was part of the initial, I think it was part of the initial vision. And maybe that came out of Fred and even myself and a few people that were in on some of the original conversations. I had been part of, in my lifetime, I had been part of community gardens that had individual plots. And I actually have a little piece that I've been trying to write about that. In my opinion, I think that can work.

But in my opinion what they do is set up competition. You know, I'm going to have my little plot next door to your little plot, and I'm going to see how your tomatoes are doing. And it also offers an opportunity for theft. You know, I go down there and I see that you're never there and you've got really great tomatoes, I just may go and take some of your tomatoes. I mean I think there's a lot of…I don't think we ever even considered the possibility of doing individual plots. I don't think that idea ever even came into our mind. I think it was just from the beginning kind of the theological, faith-based kind of idea of this place was this kind of communal thing where the whole community could come together and work on a common…

Bryan: *Right. Do you think that is duplicable without a garden manager? Or that kind of thing…I'm just wondering about the practicality of how do you decide then, "Is it carrots this year?"*

Grace: Well the board can do that. I think a board can do that, yeah. Definitely. I think your board would serve as your garden manager. And you would have a Spring and Fall community meeting and say, "What are things we want to grow?" And there needs to be somebody with some knowledge of how to rotate crops and that kind of thing. But I think it's possible. I mean I know it's possible because I know there are other churches that do it. And so they'll have a team that just helps make those decisions. We grew, the second or third year, we started growing more tomatillas and hot peppers and cilantro because of the Latino group that said, "We want more of this." Fred was really in the first year, really wanted to do a lot of heritage things. And you know people really didn't want blue potatoes; I mean blue potatoes are a gourmet kind of a thing. And people wanted collards, you know, and sweet potatoes, and so after we started…after the first year or so we started listening to what people wanted. And that was how the berries, you know we started growing blueberries. Somebody donated those plants because they thought we should have berries.

Bryan: *Maybe just two more questions that come from that. What did you do, how did you let folks know, did word just get out, or how did you get these neighbors like some of the Latino folks and some of the folks who didn't attend your church…*

Grace: We worked pretty hard at that.

Bryan: *How did you do that?*

Grace: We had someone on our board who was Latino, who was Spanish-speaking who worked at the library. And we also had a field ed student that summer, Wren Blessing, who was fluent.

And we went to, I remember Fred and I going to some of the farm worker homes. And so we went out into the community…

Bryan: *Door to door?*

Grace: Yep. Door to door. And we went to other local churches. We put up signs, but the signs never worked the same way that door to door worked. And we, Valee helped us identify people in the community that were in need of food and so we did those home visits and invited them to be part of it. I asked them if they wanted to be recipients of food. So I would say a lot happened word of mouth, but I would say within the community a lot of it was door to door kind of. And doing the community potlucks and that kind of thing and trying to invite people to come in to those. And people were skeptical when something's free. You know?

But we did these free things and tried to…we were in a program about the same time through the North Carolina Council of Churches called Living the Word. And it was two African-American churches, Missionary Baptist churches, two United Methodist (predominantly white) churches who met together for two years in a covenant group to talk about just our ministry together in the community. So that was happening at the same time. So those four churches, yeah, I mean all the right pieces falling together at the right time. Actually that's something I'd like to do at Mt. Bethel [Grace's current appointment]; that was a two year covenant that we made with each other and that was about the same time.

Bryan: *That's great. And so most of the produce from the harvest, it sounds like it went between giving it away to folks in need, giving it away to folks who gardened, and having these potlucks. Is that where most of the produce…*

Grace: Uh-huh, and then there would be excesses brought to church on Sunday and whoever wanted it could take it. I know that, I think this year the Manos kids [Obiertos Manos (Open Hands) – the youth group of the garden] have done some little c.s.a.'s [community supported agriculture shares in which people pay money at the beginning of the season and receive a box of produce each week during the growing season]. And I think this year they're actually going to go to the farmer's market.

Bryan: *That's right. Does it cost money for people to be members of the garden?*

Grace: Yes, it was five dollars a year. And I think it's still that. I don't know if they've changed it or not. But again we wanted it to be accessible to anybody. And, of course, that's a five dollar minimum; you can give as much as you want. But a five dollar membership and you only get food when you come, except for those people who are going to be delivered to. Otherwise, if you join for five dollars you have to come there to get the food. And so that was so that it would be a little bit different from a c.s.a. that you just do the work and you deliver it because part of the goal was to bring community together. So if we're going to be delivering it then it's going to prevent people from coming. And we need the work; we need your muscles.

Bryan: *Well thank you.*

Grace: I feel really, just…being away from it now I feel really privileged to have been a part of all that. It's like…people would always say, "Did you have this idea before you went there to serve?" Absolutely not. I mean I felt like the vision was a gift, and it just really blows my mind sometimes about how all of the pieces just fell together. As a matter of fact looking back on it, it seems kind of surreal; like, I lived in all of that. Somehow it doesn't seem quite… seems like I'm looking back and looking at a story that somebody's telling and I'm just a character in it.

Bryan: *Sure. Well thank you so much.*

Interpretive Excursus:

Anathoth Garden as an Embodiment of Andy Crouch's Conception of Culture Making

What is *culture*? Although connotations for the term immediately come to mind, *culture* has proven to be one of the most difficult words to define in the English language. For the purposes of his book *Culture Making: Recovering Our Creative Calling*, Andy Crouch claims, "This phrase ['making something of the world'], which I have adapted from the Christian cultural critic Ken Myers, distills what culture is and why it matters: *culture is what we make of the world*."[1] This definition is intentionally broad and ambiguous. Does, for example, this definition mean "what we make of the world" in the sense of what we produce, or does it mean "what we make of the world" in the sense of "What did you make of that movie?" – a kind of interpretive and evaluative judgment? Crouch explains later in the book that he intends the phrase to carry both of these connotations.

Fleshing out his definition further, Crouch states, "Culture is, first of all, the name for our relentless, restless human effort to take the world as it's given to us and make something else."[2] Thus, Crouch foregrounds the former connotation of what it means to make something of the world, highlighting making as *production* or *poesis*. For Crouch, then, not only is a Kandinsky painting considered to be culture, "But creation [one of the two crucial components of culture making, cultivation being the other], the marvelous making of more than was there before, also happens when a chef makes an omelet, when a carpenter makes a chair, when a toddler makes a snow angel."[3] Culture making is therefore not confined to poets, celebrities or to artistic elites. Rather,

---

1. Andy Crouch, *Culture Making: Recovering Our Creative Calling* (Downers Grove, Ill.: Intervarsity Press, 2008), 23.

2. Ibid.

3. Ibid.

Crouch's definition offers a kind of egalitarian view in which all people create culture through what they make of the world.

So what is the relationship between cultivation and creation and how does this distinction flavor Crouch's conception of culture making? Defining his trope of cultivation, Crouch asserts, "We cannot make culture without culture. And this means that *creation begins with cultivation* – taking care of the good things that culture has already handed on to us. The first responsibility of culture makers is not to make something new but to become fluent in the cultural tradition to which we are responsible. Before we can be culture makers, we must be culture keepers."[4] Because humans are not God, we never create *ex nihilo*. Indeed, all human creating is contingent upon having learned cultural practices that have been handed down to us by our elders.

But what do these cultural practices look like? To what specifically is Crouch referring when he talks about cultivation, imitation or culture keeping? Recognizing that children do express a creative drive early on, Crouch explains, "But childhood is much more fundamentally about *imitation* than *creation*. Learning language, learning our culture's vast store of stories and sayings and symbols, learning the meaning of street signs and stop lights, learning the rules of baseball, learning to jump a rope and dribble a basketball – none of these are, strictly speaking, acts of culture making. But they are indispensable acts of culture keeping, and they are necessary if the child is ever to grow up to contribute something to that cultural realm." [5] Thus, cultivation or culture keeping names the learning and carrying forth of the most basic forms of sociality. For example, then, Crouch's claim that a carpenter making a chair is a form of creation or culture making depends upon the more primary cultivation or culture keeping of learning what a chair is used for, what a saw is used for, the aesthetics of indoor furniture versus outdoor furniture, etc.

Given these definitions of culture keeping and culture making, of cultivation and creation, how do these conceptions inform

4. Ibid, 74–5.
5. Ibid, 76.

or help to make sense of the purpose and the goals of church-sponsored or Christ-centered community gardening? First, given Crouch's definitions of the terms, it is clear that church-sponsored community gardening in general and a garden like Anathoth in particular fall under the *creation* category rather than *cultivation*. With a church-sponsored community garden, a new thing is being made from what was given, namely, a plot of earth, some tools, some seeds, human labor, the sun, the rain, etc. But as human creation, a church-sponsored community garden is not *ex nihilo* but rather follows from a tradition of over one hundred years of urban gardening and community gardening in various forms in the United States. It follows from the basic skills of gardening, for example, that were cultivated in backyard gardens by the members of the church or the larger community who started the garden. It follows also from a tradition of practices of local churches seeking a vehicle for engaging nearby residents and for feeding the hungry.

In the case of Anathoth Community Garden specifically, one discovers the kinds of cultivation named in the paragraph above. But the way in which Anathoth was created and the way in which it serves as an iteration of culture making is significant. One could read the story of Anathoth as one in which the sum is much greater than its individual parts. The way in which Anathoth has taken what was given, namely, the murder, the five acre donation, the community's yearning for healing, the ideas of the pastor, and turned it into the garden of healing it is today truly exemplifies the kind of creation to which Crouch refers.

And yet, given the helpfulness of Crouch's understanding of culture making, one is left to wonder with any given instantiation of culture making, "Just *what kind* of culture is being made?" The breadth of Crouch's definition of culture making precludes the possibility that one answer would apply to the entirety of cultural production. Indeed, the recognition of a particular practice as culture making then begs this secondary question as to the kind of culture that is being created. With regards to the Anathoth Community Garden, a fitting answer to that question would involve the concept of radical hospitality. In other words, the kind of culture that is being created at Anathoth Community Garden is one in which radical hospitality norms the patterns of possibility that underwrite the daily functioning of the garden.

As the case-study of Anathoth has hopefully made clear, the kind of culture being produced at Anathoth is one marked by a radical hospitality in which the reconciliation of old divisions is taking root. Racial divisions are being healed as black, white and Hispanic gardeners work and fellowship together. People who have been welcomed to garden at Anathoth have in turn started showing up at Cedar Grove United Methodist Church for worship. Indeed, it would not be a stretch to assert that Anathoth Community Garden has affected the culture of the small town of Cedar Grove. Indeed, the Rev. Grace Hackney, Fred Bahnson, Senobia Taylor and the other persons responsible for the creation and flourishing of Anathoth Community Garden have all had a hand in making something beautiful out of the dirt they were given.

Full view of the Georgetown College Community Garden from
Clayton Street. Photographer: Amanda Langlands

View of the Georgetown College Community Garden from the back
of the garden on the west side. Photographer: Amanda Langlands

View of the Georgetown College Community Garden from the back of the garden on the east side. The raised bed in the foreground has a border of field stone that was removed from the soil that is now the vegetable garden. As you will see later, some of this field stone also made its way over to the Allelon Community Garden for the vegetable garden border there. Photographer: Amanda Langlands

This wood swing and the Adirondack chairs were donated to the Garden by a Georgetown College employee.
Photographer: Amanda Langlands

Rear view of the vegetable garden. The homes pictured across the street do not have much room in their backyards, and so a couple of these neighbors have been involved with this community garden.
Photographer: Amanda Langlands

Green peppers. Photographer: Amanda Langlands

Collards. Photographer: Amanda Langlands

A row of raspberries near the street. Behind the raspberries is our small fruit tree orchard. We chose to plant an orchard rather than another vegetable garden plot with hopes that the fruit would be ready for harvest in the Fall when our full student body is on campus so that they could help harvest and enjoy the produce. Photographer: Amanda Langlands

Pear Tree. Photographer: Amanda Langlands

Cherry Tree. Photographer: Amanda Langlands

Cultivating Neighborhood

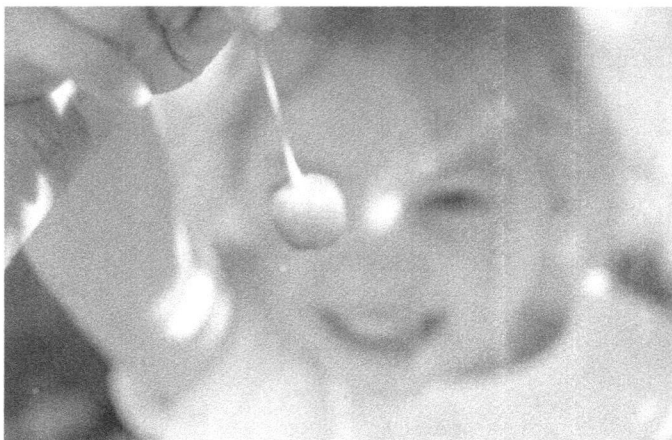

Photographer: Amanda Langlands

CHAPTER THREE

Cultivating Learning

Interview with Dr. Homer White on the Origins of the Community Garden at Georgetown College, Georgetown, Kentucky

Second Case Study

Interview Date: 2/15/11

An Interview with Dr. Homer White

Bryan: *Before coming to Georgetown you told me that you once considered becoming a Jesuit priest, and I was wondering if you could describe how your background in Jesuit spirituality, how that connects with your interest in launching community gardens.*

Homer: Well, I'd say most major Catholic religious orders have some kind of take on the right relationship between the human person and creation. So monastic orders you'll find just as interested these days in things like organic gardening, environmental concerns, and so on, as any of the newer religious orders like the Jesuits or the mendicant orders like the Franciscans. But the take of these newer orders is a little different; it's more active. In particular, Jesuit spirituality focuses on finding God in all things, not just in quiet contemplation. In fact they strive for what they call contemplation in action. There are no cloistered Jesuits; they are all in the world. They're engaged in active careers, busy careers, practical careers, finding God in everything that they meet through their work. I think this leads to their interest in social justice.

When Catholic theologians first began a century or so ago to evolve the notion of structural sin, and when popes began writing encyclicals about social justice, the Jesuits were among the first religious to take up these new perspectives and to develop very active, even very radical, peace and justice ministries. And that continues to this day; it's one of the defining marks of most Jesuits. So you can expect that anybody who's had some contact with Jesuit spirituality to get the idea that community gardening and issues about slow foods are things of abiding interest. So I think that's the Jesuit connection.

Bryan: *Sure. Before coming to Georgetown you also had a background of working with the Catholic Worker House in Washington D.C. Maybe similarly you could describe how that background connects with your interest in starting community gardens.*

Homer: I was advised out of the Jesuits and into the Catholic Worker by a man named Phillip Berrigan who was a radical peace activist. And had some friends, disciples as it were, who were young Jesuits and having a lot of trouble doing all of the civil disobedience that that kind of life demanded, reconciling that with the demands of obedience to a superior. And he thought that most young folks would be better off as lay people, more free to follow their conscience in peace matters. So I went into the Catholic Worker.

Now most people associate the Catholic Worker with soup kitchens and shelters and works of mercy. But one of the founders of the Catholic Worker was Peter Maurin. He in fact is the person who inspired Dorothy Day to begin the movement. And Peter was a French peasant from a family that had been on the land for time out-of-mind, hundreds of years in southern France. So he carried with him throughout his life an interest in the land. And he thought the solution to unemployment, (now remember the Catholic Worker was begun in the Great Depression) the solution to unemployment was a return to the land. He also thought that a return to the land would connect us to deep, traditional values in Catholicism, would connect us to creation. And so Catholic Workers started up, in addition to their soup kitchens and shelters and houses of hospitality, they started communal farms. And although these have not been the most numerous of Catholic Worker houses and not the most successful (there is a joke that Catholic Worker farms contain no Catholics, no workers and no farmers…so what do they raise? money). Still, it's in the background of Catholic Worker thought.

When I was at the Catholic Worker in Washington D.C. in 1988 I picked off the bookshelf a book by Wendell Berry (I'd never heard of him before); it's called *What are People for?* And when I read those collections of essays I said, "That man has it right." And so my interest in agriculture, slow foods, gardening, communal farms has stayed with me since then. I should point out though that it didn't all come from like books and ideas, like the idea of Jesuit spirituality or reading Jesuit books or reading Wendell Berry or reading Peter Maurin's *Easy Essays*.

The fact is also my wife has always kept a garden and so I was gardening with my wife since before we even got married. And she enjoys cooking, and she enjoys cooking from the garden. And so the reason I think I've kept at it over the years may have more to do with that than with any ideas I've got. And frankly I think that's actually kind of important in the idea of creation-centered spirituality is that you don't actually get your abiding commitments primarily from ideas. Maybe you primarily get them from gut-level kinds of background and commitments that come from particular people and particular places, because that's how you really center yourself on creation. You don't have an idea and then look around for a way to practice it; you have a practice and a life that you pay attention to.

Bryan: *That makes sense to me. That makes sense.*

Homer: But that's the idea, anyway.

Bryan: *When did you first come up with idea of trying to start a community garden here at Georgetown College?*

Homer: It was in the summer of 2008. At that point we knew there was a new sociologist who was going to be coming to Georgetown College. His name is Will Samson, and he has quite a background in sustainable communities. He brought the Sustainable Communities minor to the College. And his work in sustainable communities has typically centered around environmental concerns and community gardens as a way of building up communities. So, I wanted to do something to get the campus more active in environmental concerns, something to be kind of like a welcome mat for Will. Something for him to maybe use for students in classes. And several other people had the same feeling, that maybe a community garden would be the thing to start. So that was the genesis of the idea. I presume you're going to ask maybe what the difficulties were, getting started.

Bryan: *Yes, in the early stages and then what were the difficulties or obstacles that ended up...*

Homer: Well, the difficulty in the early stage was due to just a wrong approach on our part. We decided that for there to be a community garden, the institution, the college, had to really back it. So, you know we asked for a plot of land, we asked for the possibility of a staff member being assigned to at least part-time manage the garden, for some portion of the college budget to be devoted to getting equipment and so forth. And, our college is perennially strapped for resources so the answer was "no." And we left it alone then for almost a year.

But then we had another look at it in 2009. In the summer of 2009 Emily Brandon, who heads up International Programs, had called together a number of folks who were involved in Student Life and extracurricular groups and service groups together for a series of meetings that summer so that we could kind of connect together and streamline things and not duplicate too much work and develop some kind of synergy from their efforts. And out of those conversations the idea of starting a community garden emerged again. But this time we decided that we would just do it and not really wait for funding. But just see if we could kind of manage it on our own.

So we talked to the College and got a big lot this time, which was smaller than we had initially arranged. Just a vacant lot, and got permission to use it. And then we looked around for help in any corner we could find. I called in every friendship that I've got on the campus. People in Maintenance are my friends and they, some of them are interested in gardening. People in Campus Safety are interested in gardening, and so when help was needed, when we needed plowing, *it emerged*. When we needed to hook up water lines, *it emerged*. And so the College is actually funding the community garden, it just doesn't know that it is. It's not a line-item on the budget.

Bryan: *Sure.*

Homer: When we began to plant and I started needing to be reimbursed for things I would just pass the hat around to department chairs, for any department that had some interest in the garden. Where, you know, a class is taught in that department that maybe is going to do a service project in the garden. You go to that department chair and they would kick in fifty bucks, a hundred bucks. Had a fundraising campaign where individuals made donations. So we've really raised all of our money that way through just small donations by departments and by individuals and by groups on campus that have an interest. I'd single out maybe the Green Team, the student environmental group, as being the most helpful, in financial terms. They have contributed the money to buy the shed, the tool shed. And they're talking this year about funding the purchase of a roto-tiller.

So things like that have kept the garden functioning on the level that we can really handle. I have sought grants in the past. We've had some…we've written grants and not received them. We've gotten some tiny amount of help from Wal-Mart – one or two truckloads of discarded mulch and compost. But most of it is just totally grassroots and non-corporate.

Bryan: *Tell me about the decision-making process as far as whether there was going to be individual plots, or whether the whole thing would have just been communally gardened, or…maybe walk me through that process.*

Homer: Well…we wanted to make the garden have as many connections as possible, to as many things as possible, on-campus and off. And we thought that maybe the best way to do that would be to divide it into plots, and have one plot for Campus Ministry, one plot for the nutrition class in the KHS Department, a plot for the Sustainable Communities minor, a plot for the neighbors across the street who had been so interested in the garden and so helpful in the early stages of it. A plot maybe for the Montessori School around the corner, that if groups had their own plots then they'd be more committed to the work of the garden, having that kind of ownership. So that's how we got the plot idea, and that's how we ran the garden for its first year.

Bryan: *And how successful was that? Or maybe what did you learn from that? And after the first year, what's it going to look like for the second year?*

Homer: Well I think plots were useful in getting people involved. But once people got involved it didn't really matter to them what plot they had their hands in at any given moment. You know, folks were quite willing to do some weeding for a plot that wasn't theirs. They didn't particularly mind who picked off of their own plot. So, we think maybe plot ownership in the long run is not that important. Another problem with plot ownership is that most of these groups, the numbers are just not here in the summer. That's when most of the garden work needs to be done. So you need a small set of volunteers to see the garden through the summer anyway; they're working on all the plots. So in our second year of operation we're going to go just totally communal; as a group we decide what's going to be planted. As a group we plant and raise, and as a group we distribute the food.

Bryan: *What would you say surprised you the most after working with this garden for one year?*

Homer: That the soil was actually pretty good. That was a real big shock. It was, each plot lay over the foundations of old houses. And I really wanted this vacant lot; it was very well located right on the edge of campus so we could have connections with the community but still many students would pass it. It's a beautiful area, but it is really rocky soil. We had to remove those foundations by hand; it took months in the Fall of 2009. And the soil that was left over just looked awful. We put several truckloads of compost on it though, and it turned out to be amazingly productive for most of the vegetables that we tried. So that was the big surprise. I guess I was also surprised how tomatoes will get out of control if you don't keep up with staking them. It was a jungle.

Bryan: *Yes it was. Well maybe one other thing. What would you say you learned, something that the garden taught you this year? And it could be the garden itself or just interacting with people there or maybe just one big thing that you learned this year through your work with the garden.*

Homer: Well I think I've learned to be more grateful for the friends and relationships that I have, in my life, here at the College, because there's just been so much help from so many quarters.

Bryan: *That's wonderful and that also touches back with the Jesuit spirituality in which, I don't know a whole lot about it, but from what I do know that gratitude is an important part of Jesuit spirituality, the Daily Examen.*

Homer: Yeah, you look out at the world and you just sort of coldly evaluate…how many acts of love are required to just keep it from falling apart. And when you realize that the world is not falling apart, in fact generally it seems to be getting better, then you know that there's more than enough of these required acts of love. You've got everything required and to stare, that there's all of these acts of generosity and love and sacrifice just running around all the time, all around you, in your life, in everybody's life. How can you not be grateful?

Bryan: *What would you say is, just thinking about maybe some learning goals for students and others who may participated in the garden, what are maybe some of the things that you hope that participants learned from participating in the garden from this past year?*

Homer: Well basic things. It's always a surprise to find that folks don't know what a vegetable looks like or how it's different from a weed. You know, just knowing what a pepper is, or what a tomato is. Realizing that the thing just tastes better to you if you've been involved in the act of growing it. That has a huge impact on just the way you eat, your diet. You're going to be much more likely to eat well if you grow your own food. You're going to be much more likely to be grateful and appreciate things if you grow your own food. You're just going to enjoy a kind of a slowed-down approach to life if you eat your own food. And you don't have to eat very many of your own tomatoes to get that, to get that feel. Students start to get that feel just from one or two outings, two or three vegetables in their mouths.

Bryan: *That reminds me that one of the things I learned in the past year is the importance of relationships in general when I think about spirituality. In my tradition you know we talk a lot about having a relationship with God and certainly relationships with other people. And the connection I made this year was connecting that with food in that the more relationship I have with the food both in its production and in its preparation, as you say the more I enjoy it and in a sense connecting the food and the spirituality and sacramentality, the holier the meal is, the more sacramental it is. And then I think of the opposite of that is something like a fast-food meal where I have no relationship with the food's production, no relationship with the ones doing the preparing. And I think about my experience of eating a fast-food meal, and just all of the, what's all involved with that… drive-thrus and efficiency and speed versus the care and the slowness that you're talking about that is involved when you grow your own food and are about preparing your own food, or at least in relationship with those who are preparing the food if it's a friend or a family member, or just how different that makes the meal experience. That's a huge thing I learned this past year that was really a wonderful thing.*

Homer: I think also growing your food, eating it, talking about it with friends, figuring out what's going on in their garden, sharing a meal and talking about how you made the parts of the meal… all that's kind of a laboratory for how you approach certain tasks in life. So there's sort of two kinds of tasks: one is the kind of task where you seek a solution so that when the task is done or whatever problem you have goes away you don't have to pay attention to it anymore. You know, certain tasks that you automate with a computer I think are like this. But then there are other tasks in life, like…how about dealing with racism. If you think about it, it's the kind of thing that you don't just deal with it, solve it, shelve it, and it's gone.

I remember when I was very young, I was I think in third grade, in the very early 1970s, maybe 1971, so it was just after the civil rights movement. And my third-grade teacher, Mrs. Carter, was black, and taught us with a lot of relish the history of the civil rights movement. She was a phenomenal teacher. And you know I was listening to what was going on in class and I was reading some books at home, my parents had books like *Black Like Me* and *The Autobiography of Dick Gregory*. I was reading those books and thinking, "My goodness. Wow…we really kicked that problem! There was all this racism going on in the country and then Martin Luther King and his friends came along and they licked that problem. And it's all gone away now except for a few of my cousins back down in Georgia maybe"…you know. And I remember telling that to Mrs. Carter, and she said, "Well, Homer, I don't think it's really like that. There's a reason I'm teaching you about the civil rights movement, because it's not really like that." And I didn't agree at the time. But as I grew up I saw that she was right, that, you know, the more you think that racism is licked, that everything is all right now, the more the problem festers underneath. It's something that you have to take out every day individually, communally, and just keep on working on, taking on every day.

Food is like that. You don't want to solve the problem of food so that you don't have to think about it anymore. If you go with that solution then you're into factory-farming, and that's not sustainable, and it leads to unhappiness. I think energy is the same kind of thing. We're hooked on fossil fuels because we want to solve the energy problem so that we don't have to think and be aware and be appreciative of where energy comes from. Alternative energies are things that we're gonna have to tinker with all the time. But you know the neat thing is working with alternative energy, growing gardens, they're all fun. They bring us closer together. They're things we enjoy talking about. They're things we enjoy doing. They're things that, you know, bring us joy as we deal with those problems and get better and make progress with them. So there are some tasks that you don't really want to go away, and I think that the slow foods movement teaches us what some of those tasks are.

Bryan: *Well thank you, and I agree. I hadn't thought about it in that way but I thank you for that response. Tell me, what happens to most of the produce from the garden?*

Homer: Well like when we had a school group come over, we make sure that these children take home a tomato or two. Same for any college group. People who work in the garden regularly are encouraged to take what they want, you know, within reason, and nobody's ever been unreasonable about what they take. But by far most of the produce has gone to Scott United Ministries, to the A.M.E.N. House. During the summer about once or twice a week we would walk up a bucket of tomatoes or cucumbers to A.M.E.N. House on Main St. I think by the end we had probably given about 150 pounds of produce which really surprised me, that it's only 1500 square feet of garden that was in operation that first year.

Bryan: *Tell me, you touched on this a little bit but you talked about some of the neighbors you engaged who were really helpful in the early parts of the garden's existence. You mentioned the Montessori School and other classes. Tell me, why do you think it's important for the garden to be involved with neighbors in that way. What does that do for the garden? Why is that important?*

Homer: Well it makes the garden look organizationally like nature looks, connected to everything. That would be one reason.

Bryan: *And what did you find was the response as far as the different schools and different neighbors? Did you have to do a lot of convincing in order to get most of them involved? Were some not interested at all?*

Homer: I don't have to do a lot of convincing to get involved. You do have to stay on top of it to keep them involved. Because people are very busy and they do things like a community garden on the rump end of very demanding full-time jobs. So those few of us who are in coordination need to remember to remind folks at the

Montessori School that tomatoes are ripe and could be picked if you want to bring the school group out…try to find days and times that are good for them to do that. Same goes for groups across campus. You have to remind people each semester. Is your class a class where work in the garden could be some useful component?

Bryan: *In the midst of the garden's first growing season a decision was made to turn the eastern plot into a fruit orchard. Maybe you could speak a little bit about what prompted that decision.*

Homer: Sure. People were saying, particularly people who did a lot of work in the garden over the summer, "Wouldn't it be nice to have an orchard somewhere?" Secondly, the plot over which the orchard now stands was not under cultivation; we were still removing rocks from it. And we never did finish removing all of those rocks. So it looked like there was going to be a lot of hard work and maybe another year before we could get this to be a vegetable plot. And then number three is just that I happened to be eating an apple and thinking, "Well maybe we should just have the orchard right there." You know, the remaining rock removal was relatively trivial if you want to put in a small orchard. So we threw one in in the Fall of 2010. And that seems to be the right idea. So everything is now in one place. I hope the garden will expand across campus as time goes on. And in a sense it has expanded with Nick Babladelis putting the small plot in behind Knight Hall and with the seed-starting project getting underway across campus. But for now most of what you see is all in one spot. It's very small scale but it's diverse.

Bryan: *That kind of relates to the next question as far as what goals might you have regarding three years from now what the garden might look like as far as expansion possibly or…*

Homer: Well I think I'd like to see other elements. I'd like to see bees on-site. We're getting started with composting on east campus and that's something I hope goes well. There might be the possibility of a greenhouse someday. I think also we've had plans to work with the McCandless House, the house right next door, has a kitchen, which we've used in activities already. I think maybe installing some elements in that house that illustrates sustainable living. You know maybe some worm composting being set up inside, in the kitchen, some rain barrels on the outside that can help feed the garden. Things like that, you know just stuff that's nice, educational, demonstration things to show students and visitors to talk about how they work.

Bryan: *Obviously one of the goals of the garden has been to connect in more tangible ways part of our campus community with neighbors, not necessarily the people across the street but our neighbors in Scott County – either folks who take part in Scott United Ministries, the A.M.E.N. House, maybe someone who receives some of the food. Was the garden as successful this year as you had hoped in being able to make some of those connections between the institution and the broader community?*

Homer: Mostly. Certainly with A.M.E.N. House *yes*. I would have liked to have seen a little bit more coming and going with some of the church groups. And there's another kind of longer term dream that is slow to be realized and that's there really should be other community gardens in Georgetown, kind of in this downtown area. There should be a network someday. I hope that, for example, Faith Baptist gets its community garden going. I hope Georgetown Baptist can maybe take a currently unused plot of land from the College and have a garden of their own. If there's a network I think things would just run together better and it would be a way of sharing resources.

And getting back to the Catholic Worker a little bit. In Lexington the Catholic Action Center, which serves the homeless and which was founded on Catholic Worker principles, has really made a connection between service to the homeless, the working mercy, and the back-to-the-land movement through community gardening. They have a large community garden out on the Bluegrass Technical Community College campus. They have a large, commercial worm composting operation. And these operations are run, staffed by volunteers and by folks who are served by the Catholic Action Center: homeless folks, folks coming off of addictions to drugs and alcohol find it very therapeutic to work in the garden and to see the work of their hands and to see the commercial success of the composting tea operation that they've got going on (there's a worm composting tea that they sell). So, who knows? As this ministry to the homeless takes root in Georgetown maybe work in the garden can be a part, something that's available for folks that we serve as well. We'll see. We'll see how the other community gardens, the churches and the institutions that they're associated with, we'll see how that goes for them.

Bryan: *Just two more questions here. I've read recently in a book on the history of community gardening in the United States that interest in community gardening historically has always spiked during times of social crisis. So, you know the Victory Gardens, the war gardens in World War I and World War II, and the beginnings of the community garden movement in the sixties and seventies following Vietnam and civil rights and the social unrest there. I'm curious as to what thoughts you might have as to what social crisis today, if the recent interest in community gardening that I've noticed especially among persons of faith, if it is related to a social crisis, what social crisis do you think this might be a response to? Or what particular things in society today do you think this interest might be related to?*

Homer: I think it's probably two factors. One is the increasing awareness of environmental crisis through our thoughts about global warming. And secondly, I think it's people looking for a way to reconnect to the world and to each other outside of the virtual world in the real world. So it's a reaction to social networking and Facebooking, interneting, cell-phoning; attempt to find real connections.

Bryan: *And finally what has been the process of coming up with a name for the garden?*

Homer: Well we still haven't come up with a name. I've thought of a couple, but I've been slow to impose a name. Probably this Spring we'll just have a little go around by email, you know, we want to do it virtually…where people can suggest names and I'll collect them. And then I'll put them out to folks in an email and we can sort of talk a little bit more and maybe eventually…I don't know if there will be an email vote or just by conversations one name will emerge. We'll see.

Bryan: *And why do you think it's important that instead of naming it right away or imposing a name on it from day one, what's the value in allowing a year or two years to kind of shape that?*

Homer: Well first of all I don't know if there's value, there's just some tasks you find you can get away with not doing right away. But then the other thing is, you don't want the name to be too closely connected to an idea about how it's supposed to go, right? Under this creation-centered idea shouldn't the name come from something concrete about the place, about its relationship to other places or to people. So people need to be in the garden for a while and let some specific feature of the garden suggest the name rather than have some ideology suggest the name.

Bryan: *Which makes sense…the name grows with the garden, gives it time to germinate and sprout.*

Homer: Yeah. I'm not really sure why in our culture we name the children when they are born. Quite often we name them before they are born. We name them hypothetically – if it's a boy then this, if it's a girl then that. I like the idea in some other cultures where you wait around. Maybe you have a provisional name, but the people watch you. And once you do something defining then they give you a name based on that defining act.

Bryan: *Well thank you very much.*

Annual work day on the first Saturday of May to prepare the
Allelon Community Garden for the summer growing season.
Photographer: Charlie Perkins

The two raised beds in the foreground were created as a part of
an Eagle Scout Project by a youth member of Faith Baptist Church.
The drip lines that you see are connected to a large rain barrel that
is connected to the back of the church building. The pump that
pushes the water from the rain barrel out to the raised bed (which is

about forty feet away) is powered by a small solar panel on the roof.
Photographer: Charlie Perkins

We try to involve the children of the church as much as
possible with the garden. Photographer: Charlie Perkins

The fence that we placed around the garden is intended to keep
rabbits and other small animals out. Photographer: Charlie Perkins

Photographer: Charlie Perkins

Photographer: Charlie Perkins

CHAPTER FOUR

Cultivating Neighbors

Allelon Community Garden at Faith Baptist Church, Georgetown, Kentucky

Author's Note: *Since I helped to start this Garden and have served as its coordinator for the last four years, I wrote this case-study as a participant/observer.*

THE IDEA FOR STARTING a community garden at Faith Baptist Church in Georgetown, KY was hatched well over a decade before ground was broken. Around 1995 the Church bought five home lots behind the church building in the neighborhood that adjoins the church's property. I learned from Dr. Greg Earwood, the pastor of Faith at that time, that from the very beginning a community garden was one of the ideas put forward as to what the church might do with that property. So the conversation that began in January of 2011 about starting a community garden at Faith was really a continuation of a conversation that had been going off-and-on for fifteen years. It seems that what was lacking was a small group of people who would take ownership of the project and see it through. That is where our new small group that meets on Sunday mornings comes in.

In the winter of 2010, the current pastor of Faith, Rev. Bob Fox, organized a pizza lunch to which he invited several young couples who were not already regularly involved in a Sunday School class. During the lunch, Bob led a conversation in which he gauged our interest in forming a new Sunday School class. Since everyone in the room was interested, Bob solicited the class for a volunteer or two to serve as the leader/s of this new class. Jeremiah Tudor and I volunteered to lead, and we planned to start meeting together on Sunday mornings in January of 2011.

Because of prior relationships I had with some of the members of our new Sunday School class, I trusted that there would be some interest in the possibility of our class working together to launch a community garden at the church. Over the course of a few weeks I pitched the idea to the class, and almost every couple within the class thought that it was an idea worth pursuing. I had this sense that if we were going to propose the creation of a garden to the administrative council of the church, that they would be more inclined to receive the proposal favorably if it came from an entire Sunday School class rather than from just an individual. It is also worth noting that my wife Amanda serves as the Minister to Children and Minister of Education at Faith Baptist Church. She was hired in the summer of 2010, and so we were both relative new to the church (although Amanda had been somewhat involved in the ministries of Faith as a youth).

With our yet-to-be-named Sunday School class's backing, I asked Pastor Bob about his thoughts about us starting a community garden. He said that he was all for it and he helped me to understand the process that would need to take place before such a thing could be approved. First, he explained, I would need to attend the next Trustee meeting, talk to them about the idea, answer any questions they might have, and procure their blessing to move forward. After that, he suggested that we have an information meeting about the proposal following an upcoming church potluck lunch. This meeting would serve: to educate interested persons about the reasons for starting a community garden, to answer any questions and to talk about any objections that church members may have had, and to start a list of people who, alongside our Sunday School Class, might be interested in participating in the work of the garden. After that meeting, Pastor Bob, continued, we would need to have the garden approved at the church business meeting.

Perhaps the most important piece of advice that Pastor Bob asked me at that point of the process had to do with finances. He said, "If there is a way for you all to start the garden without asking the church for any money, I think you'll have a much easier time getting it approved." I assured him that I had every intention of making this garden *budget neutral.* That was a term and a strategy that I had adopted as a result of my experience in helping to launch the community garden at Georgetown College. With the fiscal challenges that colleges, churches and most non-profits have experienced since the economic downturn of 2008, I knew that money was tight and that organizations are generally looking for ways to cut costs and to increase revenues, and NOT looking to take on additional expenditures. Our experience at Georgetown College taught me that it is much easier and wiser to start a garden and to solicit donations (both financial and in-kind donations of seeds, gardening equipment, compost, etc.) than it is to wait to start until the garden is given a line-item in the organization's budget. The wonderful thing is that it does not cost very much money to start a garden, and if there is enough interest then participants tend to provide what is needed for the work to get accomplished.

That financial question being Pastor Bob's only vocalized concern, he called the Chairman of the Trustees later that week to get this garden request placed on their upcoming meeting's agenda. Their next meeting was scheduled for early March, 2011, and they accepted Pastor Bob's request to add this garden proposal to their agenda. The conversation with the Trustees went well. They asked several questions about the specifics and logistics of the proposed garden. They inquired as to who would be in charge of it? I told them that I would be willing to serve as the coordinator.

They asked about who would be doing the work? I let them know that most of the members of our new Sunday School class were interested in helping out, but that we would also be working hard to get others (both church members and non-church member neighbors) involved. They inquired as to where on the property we would put the garden and how big were we planning to make it? I told them that we were planning to start small, something like one or two plots measuring approximately 10' X 15'. I explained that we didn't know exactly where we would put those plots, and that I was open to their suggestions.

Since we had recently found some discarded drug paraphernalia behind the church building there was a concern expressed about the possibility of vandalism. I believe I shared a response that one of our Sunday School class members, Dr. Jonathan Sands Wise, mentioned when that concern was brought up in our Sunday School conversation about this issue. He said, "I don't think we have to worry about teenagers vandalizing the garden. Most teenagers are scared of vegetables because they don't know what they are." Moreover, my lack of concern about vandalism largely stemmed from a conversation I had had with a man who oversaw a community youth garden outside of the Ed Davis center in Georgetown, KY. This center serves the educational and recreational needs of a lower-income community in town. The director of the Ed Davis center at that time, Terry, told me that the youth never vandalized their garden because they knew their mothers might be asking them to go and to pick some tomatoes out of it that night to serve up for dinner. That anecdote both challenged me to plan to get neighborhood youth involved in the work of our proposed garden and gave me confidence that vandalism should not be a huge concern of ours.

Another concern that was raised by one of the Trustees (and this was a concern that was echoed by other members of the church in casual conversations about the garden proposal) was that the soil would not be any good. The man had good reason to believe that the soil would not be lush. The five home lots that comprised the field behind the church building where we were planning to start the garden are surrounded by homes of a subdivision called Bradford Place. This subdivision was built within the last 25 years on what used to be a farm. Although I do not know the extent of what was grown on that farm, I have heard that they did raise cattle. Whereas much of that farm land therefore had soil that would have been healthy, the standard practice of builders in subdivisions like Bradford Place is to remove all of the topsoil on a lot before they begin building. In a conversation about this practice, one church member who witnessed the construction of the subdivision described the removal of all that topsoil as "the raping of the land." Although I did not live in that subdivision, I lived in a similar one at the time. After digging up the grass to start a garden in my own backyard, I could attest to the frustration of having very little topsoil underneath the sod. Rather, I had a rocky clay to work with that needed to be amended in order to produce well.

Thus, because those five lots were a part of that subdivision the Trustee assumed that the builders would have taken off the topsoil of the lots owned by the church even though homes were never built on them. At the time of that meeting, I had not yet dug around back in those lots and so I did not know the condition of the soil. However, I attempted to assuage his concerns with two comments. First, I mentioned that if the soil is bad we could always amend the soil and/or build raised beds. The expenses to do that would rise, but it was an option. Secondly, and more importantly, I explained what I take to be a crucial and fundamental principle for Christ-centered community gardening, namely, that we would be under no pressure to produce a certain amount of vegetables. We had no quota to meet, and maximizing yield was not a priority for us. In this way, Christ-centered community gardening resists our cultural impulses for productivity and efficiency – for getting things done so that we can check them off of our to-do lists. Rather, I explained, it is the process that matters most; the relationships that are built and strengthened through the shared fun and shared labor of getting hands in the dirt together. So, even if the soil was terrible, I reasoned, that would not stymie our efforts. Instead, such an obstacle would become one of the first challenges that we would have to figure out together how to overcome.

The final concern that we discussed had to do with water. I asked the Trustees what their thoughts were regarding how we should go about watering the garden during the hot and dry months of July and August. We discussed whether it would be best to have the water company put a new water line out near the garden or whether it would be best for us to run a hose from an existing spigot on the back of the church building. The problem with the former option was that it would have cost about $1400 to have the water company do that installation. We obviously did not have that kind of money on hand. It would have been possible for us to fundraise that amount, but we were hesitant about launching things with such a huge expense. The second option of using the existing spigot was a more attractive option to me, but there were concerns over that option as well. I told the Trustees early in the meeting that my plan and goal was for the garden to be budget-neutral. Any expenses, I explained, that the garden had would be contributed by garden participants through the establishment of a separate garden account that we were going to ask the church to create for us.

However, if the garden was going to be using the church's water line, thus increasing the church's water bill, we all realized that that could get complicated (especially when we were promoting the garden as a budget-neutral activity). One option we discussed involved figuring out what the average monthly water bill was for the church, and then whatever overage there was during the months that we used the church's water could be paid for from the garden account. When I discovered during that meeting that the church's monthly water was only around $30-$40, I proposed that instead of paying the overage, the garden could pay the entire water bill for the church during the summer months. That proposal and the conversation overall seemed to satisfy the Trustees that the water issue could be figured out, and that it should not be an obstacle for the creation of the garden.

At the end of the Trustee meeting I was very encouraged. The Trustees told me that they would bless our efforts and that if we needed help they would be willing to do what they could to support us. Thus, I talked to Pastor Bob again and we scheduled a community garden information/interest meeting following a potluck lunch that was already scheduled for after morning worship on an upcoming Sunday. I was thrilled that 15 people showed up to the meeting that day and we had a terrific conversation. As I had for the Trustees, I explained to this group the basics of why we were hoping to launch a community garden and sought to answer any questions that they had. I also had an information sheet that I passed out to each participant. One of the most interesting questions that we ended up discussing stemmed from a question someone asked, "What happens if someone comes in and steals the vegetables?" This question led to a discussion about hunger in our town and the role of the church. One of the points I made was that we were planning to give the vast majority of our produce away to our local food bank anyways, so if someone comes in and *steals* something they would be simply saving us some harvesting labor!

Based on another question I received, I was able to bring up the very important question of what *success* means with regards to a church-sponsored community garden. How would we know if we were being successful? One helpful way to approach that question is to consider its opposite. It is perhaps a bit more obvious what *failure* would look like for a community garden; namely, it would be one in which nobody participated. From there, we talked a bit about what success might look like. First, it would not involve a certain amount of produce, especially in the garden's first year of operation. Rather, success for a church-sponsored community garden ought to be measured in terms of: the amount of participation both from church members and from non-church member neighbors, the extent to which interpersonal and intergenerational relationships are deepened and enriched, the extent to which gardening novices (including youth) are apprenticed into the skills of growing one's own food and stewarding the land well, and the extent to which the garden can become a teaching tool to broaden one's depth of understanding and appreciation for the Bible and for the miracle of creation. Another thing we discussed was the need to have regularly scheduled meetings (monthly, perhaps) in which we would talk about the garden and make the decisions that needed to be made.

During this meeting I passed around a sheet inviting interested persons to put down their names and email addresses so that I could add them to an email distribution list that I would be creating for the garden. I was excited to see at the conclusion of that meeting that twelve people had signed up. Although many of the folks who attended this meeting and who signed up to be on the email distribution list were members of our Sunday School class, the majority of those present were not and several of the people who signed up to be on the email list were not. Whereas most of the conversation about the garden had taken place previously with our Sunday School class during our Sunday School hour, with this expansion of interest moving our conversations online seemed like the logical thing to do. Through these emails we would share information about the needs of the garden, solicit donations of money or labor from people as those needs arose, and brainstorm ideas about how to continue to make things better. Along with the core contingent of our Sunday School class, it seemed that we also had enough broader buy-in that we felt very encouraged to move forward.

The final step in the approval process involved getting the garden proposal passed through the business meeting. I arrived at this Sunday evening meeting with revised copies of the information sheet that I had used at the Trustees meeting and at our informational/interest meeting.[1] The revisions of that information sheet were based on the comments and questions I had received at those previous meetings. For the business meeting I was invited to give a three minute presentation on the garden proposal, and with that time I attempted to stress the *why* of the garden; how, for example, the garden would connect with the mission of the church

1. A copy of this sheet is included in Appendix A.

and our outreach priorities. At the end of my short presentation I opened up the floor for questions, but there were not any questions raised. Quickly, a vote was taken and the motion passed without a single *no* vote.

We were therefore free to proceed with our plans for the garden. The next step, we decided, would be to have a *consecration of the soil* service over the garden following our Palm Sunday morning service (which was a few weeks away on April 17, 2011). Before that service happened, our Sunday School class decided it would be good for a few of us to meet on a Wednesday night and to decide where exactly we were going to put the garden. The night we met we carried our shovels out back behind the church building, spending a few minutes talking about where the best spot might be based on proximity to the water source, general aesthetics of space, etc. When we came to a provisional decision, we decided ceremonially to go ahead and to turn over the first shovel of soil. We had no idea before we dug that first shovel down what the soil would be like, whether it would be hard and rocky or soft and lush. Fortunately, when we turned over that first bit of soil, the dirt looked and felt healthy and loamy. Since there was neither rock nor clay in sight, we concluded that the home builders of that neighborhood must have never scraped the topsoil off of the spot where we had decided to start the garden. Indeed, later when we tilled the soil for the two garden plots, we ran across only a couple of field stones (which is very unusual for our limestone/calcium-rich soil). This experience of grace typified many of the ways in which things came together in the Spring of 2011 to make this garden launch successful.

Looking at the calendar past the garden consecration service, we noted that the church had already planned a community-wide Mission Blitz for the morning of the first Saturday in May (Kentucky Derby day, a big deal around here). During these three hours many folks from the church volunteer to serve in a number of different ways both in and around the church building and out in the Georgetown community. We decided that that would be a great opportunity for us to recruit volunteers to get the garden started.

So, we marked off the two plots in which we were going to grow vegetables. Although our mantra all along had been *start small* and we had been planning to start with just one plot, the youth of the church had just spent a week on their Alternative Spring Break trip working and learning at Anathoth Community Garden in Cedar Grove, NC. So they came back excited about gardening and pledged to help over the summer. That gave us the confidence to plan out two plots instead of the one we had originally planned.

One of the conversations that we had been having all along had to with the decision we had to make as to whether we would only have plots that would be farmed communally or instead create individual plots for people to pledge to husband. For months off and on we discussed the relative merits of both of these options. I knew that some community gardens did it one way and some did it the other way, and so we tried to figure out what would make the most sense for us given the specifics of our context. After much thought and conversation we decided that we would *start small* and just have the two plots that would be farmed communally. Our hope was that later on as more and more people got involved, that we could grow towards having some individual plots if there were requests for that. I knew through my experience helping to launch the community garden at Georgetown College that although we had started out the first year with different groups pledging to take care of individual plots, by the end of the summer it ended up functioning much more communally. Partly that was because although some groups had pledged to take care of a plot, as the summer wore on that group's volunteers came less and less frequently. So, the committed core group of gardeners ended up taking care of all of the plots and we paid less and less attention to whose plot was whose. The only exception to that with the Georgetown College community garden was that the front plot was well taken care of by the folks who lived across the street, and so we admired their careful work and left their plot alone.

The Mission Blitz/Garden launch was a great success. We had approximately ten adults and six youth helping us that day. In a short amount of time we were able to haul in several loads of compost and mulch, till up the soil, and pick up a couple of truck-bed loads of field-stone from the pile that had been created when we cleared the soil at the Georgetown College community garden and use them as a border for the plots. Mission Blitz officially concluded with a lunch in the church's Family Life Center. Although most of the participants left after lunch a few of us stuck around to spread the mulch and to put away all of the tools we had used. Whereas the compost had been dumped into the plots and tilled in, the mulch was placed around the border of the garden plots in order to help control weeds. The mulch and the stone border greatly enhanced the aesthetics of our garden space.

We decided that we would have two group gardening nights each week over the course of the summer. Since folks were used to coming up to the church building on Sunday and/or Wednesday nights anyways, we decided that those two nights starting at 6:30 pm would be our weekly group work nights. Sundays and Wednesdays were also good choices because if we would have chosen to meet on Saturdays and Sundays, for example, that would have left open the possibility that the garden would go five days without water, weeding or harvesting. Ensuring that someone will be working in the garden at least once every three-four days is crucial, especially during times of dry weather and harvest. Although anyone could certainly come and work anytime, garden members could usually count on there being other people there to work and fellowship with during those designated times. We also tried to divide it up so that none of the garden leaders (the two or three of us who were the most committed and had enough gardening experience to be able to lead the gardeners who showed up that night) were expected to be there both nights each week.

In the previous paragraph I referred to *garden members,* but I have not yet explained our conception of what garden membership involved. We had some conversation through email and during our Sunday School conversations about this, but we never did define very clearly what it meant to be a member of this church-sponsored community garden. This conversation seemed to be more significant when we were exploring the idea of having individual plots where we knew there would be a stronger need for clear expectations and accountability to hedge against situations such as people signing up for plots but not doing anything with them, etc. But since we had decided to tend the plots communally, there was less urgency in defining things like membership, expectations, rules and regulations, etc. For that first growing season, we ended up adopting a posture of *everyone is welcome to come and to garden as much or as little as they see fit.*

As mentioned, from the beginning our hope was that we would have both members of the church and non-church member neighbors working together in the garden. But once we got going the important question, "How do you get those non-church member neighbors involved?" arose. We did not spend much time strategizing about how to get those neighbors connected to the work we were doing. As a result, we did not have very many of those neighbors involved in the work during that first summer's growing season. We did talk to neighbors as we were out there working and as they were outside doing things. We also initiated many conversations with people from the neighborhood who happened to walk by the garden. In November of 2011, after the end of the growing season, we did spend some time going door to door meeting people and handing out rack cards (narrow fliers on card stock) in the apartment complexes across the street from our church building. These rack cards described the basics of the garden and contained contact information at the bottom in case anyone was interested in working in the garden for the 2012 growing season.

Perhaps the one successful thing we did do during the summer of our first growing season to involve the neighbors was to have door-to-door free farmer's markets over in the apartment complexes. A few times I did this by myself, and a couple of times I went with one of the other gardeners. We did this during the peak of our tomato harvest. The basil was also coming in very nicely at that time, and so we gave as much basil as we could along with the tomatoes. Since many of the residents seemed unfamiliar with fresh basil, I strongly encouraged them to try a tomato, basil, mozzarella and olive oil sandwich on toast. Some wonderful conversations often ensued. Even if the neighbors chose not to take any tomatoes, they were generally very friendly with us. At least one woman even invited us into her home. She blessed us by sharing with us about her great love for God and how God had been at work in her life recently.

We did carry brochures from the church with us and we tried to give one away to everyone who was willing to take some of our tomatoes. To the best of my knowledge, none of the residents who received a brochure as a part of our free farmer's market or who received a rack card as a part of our door-to-door campaign in November (described above) has contacted us yet about joining our community garden or has visited the church for Sunday worship. Although that might be viewed as frustrating or as a kind of failure, I do not think so. Sure, it would have been great to have had greater levels of interest in the community garden from the neighbors. However, one thing I have learned is that what is most important is not the sheer numbers of people involved, but rather the depth of relationships that are being formed. As my Mother once told me, "Relationships are the hardest thing you'll ever do." Indeed, growing relationships takes time. Our hope is that through a consistent, humble and generous presence with our neighbors we will develop and strengthen some of those personal relationships. We have to continue to remind ourselves that one of the most important functions of the community garden is as a *vehicle* for relationship-building. This reminder helped me whenever I was tempted to think of success in terms of numbers, both the amount of produce harvested and/or the number of people involved in the work of the garden.

Giving away produce in this way proved to be one of the most fun aspects of community gardening for me personally. One of the key things I learned was that whereas if one is going door-to-door trying just to give away church brochures, people tend to be more reticent to talk. However, if one is giving away free, biodynamic produce that they have grown, people are much more likely to engage in conversation. Sometimes that conversation bent towards tomatoes, vegetables and healthy eating, sometimes it had to do with gardening and important people in their lives who grew a garden, and sometimes (when they found out we were from the church across the street) the conversation went straight to Jesus. Following our wonderful experiences meeting people through our door-to-door free farmer's market, I caught myself saying more than once, "If I am ever the chairperson of an evangelism committee, forget door-hangers, we're going to give away tomatoes!"

One of the most exciting developments over the course of the first growing season was the decision by one of the church's youth (Jamey) to work with our garden as his final Eagle Scout project. Especially, I appreciate the way he approached the brainstorming of his project. He had a conversation with the garden leaders and learned about what the greatest needs of the garden were at that point. We talked about having access to water being our greatest need. It was a great grace to find out that this youth's father happened to work at our city's water department, and so the ground was set for his project. After surveying the site and thinking through different possibilities, Jamey decided on a two-part project. The first part would involve digging a trench from the spigot on the back of the church building to a spot on the edge of the garden. In this trench Jamey would lay a PVC pipe which would contain a hose. This hose would run from the spigot to a new spigot that he would install on the edge of the garden. With this apparatus in place, we would be able to connect a hose to the garden spigot and thus easily be able to reach the entire garden with water. This fixture would thus prevent us from having to hook up several hoses each time that we needed to water the garden and then recoil them when we were done watering. The reason why we had to pick up the hoses after each watering was that if we were to leave the multiple hoses stretched out to the garden it would be a potential tripping hazard and it would have prevented the Trustees from being able to mow the lawn behind the church building.

The second aspect of Jamey's project involved building two raised beds next to the garden. The sides of these beds were made of wood, and each bed measured approximately 4' X 10'. Once the sides were built Jamey filled them with topsoil. He went on to plant different kinds of herbs in each bed: parsley, basil, rosemary, thyme, mint, etc. These beds and the water piping have been tremendous additions to the garden. We have truly enjoyed the energy and the vision that the youth have brought and continue to bring to this gardening project.

Another exciting development that occurred towards the end of the first growing season was the planting of our fruit orchard. In late August we purchased eleven fruit trees from a small local nursery that was just a few months away from closing down. We bought different varieties of apple trees, pear trees, and a cherry tree. The reasons for our planting an orchard were many. For example, we were excited about the possibility of harvesting fruit and about having a longer growing season with which to work (since the fruit harvest tends to be later in the season than the vegetable harvest). Also, we had learned that biodiversity is an important goal for any community garden because the more biodiverse a garden is the more it reflects nature. Finally, we also believed the trees would provide some nice shade should we ever want to install some picnic tables in the future. At the same time we also planted seven blueberry bushes of different varieties next to the raised herb beds.

The final two things I will report on with regards to the garden involve the garden's name and its mission statement. I was hesitant to push the issue of naming the garden straight away after its launch because I had been convinced by Dr. Homer White in working with him on the community garden at Georgetown College that there is something to be said about allowing a garden to grow into a name, not unlike the way in which historically Native Americans waited to name their young until the young person had *lived into* a name. However, as we continued to talk about name possibilities throughout the duration of our first growing season, a name emerged that found favor with our core volunteers. The Greek word *Allelon* was proposed and gained traction; it means "one another" and is used in the New Testament in phrases such as "love one another" and "care for one another." The possibility of this name was discussed among garden participants by email and it was adopted towards the end of the summer of our first growing season. Our hope is that this garden will inspire us to love God and to love our neighbors in service to one another.

Around the same time that we were having conversations about naming the garden we also began to think about naming its mission. What, after all, were we seeking to accomplish through the creation of this community garden? In her book *City Bountiful*, Laura Lawson concludes by noting the importance for community gardens of having specific goals that are assessable. Her point is that given the historical tendency of these gardens to be short-lived because of land development or a lack of funding, it is important that community gardens not just rely on the general feelings of good will that such gardens evoke, but that there should be research and data that demonstrates the specific goods that community gardens are producing in terms of community development, economic empowerment, therapeutic recreation, etc. Since the goods of a garden will at least partly depend on the specificities of its context, goals are important to help the garden coordinating team to know what it is they are hoping to accomplish through the garden.[2]

Although Allelon was far away from the kind of research and data that Lawson calls for, to get started I drew up a couple of different proposals for a mission statement. Then, I emailed them to our garden list and invited feedback and suggestions. The only people on the list to reply to my email were Dr. Jonathan and Elizabeth Sands Wise, the couple who (besides myself) have been the most invested in the project. After reading the suggestions that were offered, the mission statement we chose reads: *The mission of Allelon Community Garden is to serve Jesus Christ and our neighbors, and to nourish the family of Faith by cultivating Sabbath*

---

2. One important, related, and overarching question that Lawson raises in her book involves whether a community garden or an urban garden is primarily an end in itself or if it is a means or a vehicle to some other end. My sense is that a garden could be either depending on context. At least for Christ-centered community gardening, a community garden is primarily a means to the end of encountering Christ and witnessing faithfully to the Kingdom he proclaimed.

*relationships among church members and those around us, by being
a teaching tool for Christian formation, and by growing healthy food
for the hungry and for the enjoyment of all.*

There are a couple of things worth noting regarding this
statement. First, it begins with the main thing for disciples of Jesus Christ, the greatest commandment. Our hope is that the love
of God and neighbor grounds any church-based initiative within
the greater community, and for that reason it made sense to begin
our mission there. Secondly, the phrase "the cultivation of Sabbath
relationships" requires some explication. By Sabbath relationships,
we mean the kind of relationships that have at their core an appreciation for and a mutual encouragement towards a rhythm of life
that balances work, rest and play in a God-honoring way.

Finally, I offer a word about the didactic function of the garden and its relationship to Christian formation. When we describe
the garden as a teaching tool we remember that historically Israel
had an agrarian culture. Indeed, one finds in the teachings of Jesus Christ numerous references to agriculture. Our hope is that
introducing non-gardeners to gardening will, for example, help
them to experience the difference between rocky, weed-choked
soil and the good soil that Jesus described (Mark 4:3–8). One may,
for example, have heard all of their life in church that "the harvest
is plentiful but the laborers are few," (Matthew 9:37) but this verse
takes on new meaning to a person who is in the garden alone on a
warm August evening because some of her fellow gardeners went
on vacation during the peak harvest time for the cherry tomato
plants! Our hope is that through gardening participants will be
able to experience the Word afresh in deeper and in more revela-
tory ways.

Earlier in this case study I noted that one of the questions we
wrestled with in our preliminary conversations about the garden
involved, How would we know if our garden was successful? What
does success mean for a church-sponsored community garden?
And how do we assess what the corporate impact of the garden
has been? Thinking about these questions at the end of our first
growing season, I decided to send out an email to our Allelon

distribution list in November of 2011 that described the fruit of our work together. Some of the results listed are assessable items such as the approximate yield of vegetables. But I also included some anecdotal highlights to help round out the numbers. That email reads:

> Dear Friends,
>
> I wanted to share with you all some good news. I did some end of the year tabulatin' for the Allelon Community Garden at Faith. Here are the numbers I have regarding what we gave away to the AMEN House:
>
> 17 lbs. - green peppers; 8 lbs. – lettuce; 4 lbs. – onion; 30 lbs. – squash; 5 lbs. - bush beans; 3 lbs. – basil; 3 lbs. – carrots; 218 lbs. - tomatoes
>
> My best guess is that we gave away approximately 18 lbs. worth of tomatoes and 1lb. of basil door-to-door to our neighbors in the apartments across the street. Regarding the produce both given away to church members on Sunday mornings and that taken home by garden participants as we gardened, I'm going to put a rough guess on that amount at 50 lbs. (no way of knowing for sure) If you exclude that 50 lbs., that means that we gave away more than 307 lbs. of fresh (basically organic) produce to our neighbors here in Scott County! That is worth celebrating!
>
> THANK YOU ALL FOR YOUR SUPPORT THROUGH OUR FIRST YEAR OF COMMUNITY-GARDENING AT FAITH! For some of you that support involved words of encouragement, for some it involved financial support, for some it involved many hours of sweat working on our little patch of good soil. However you were involved this year, I THANK YOU FROM THE BOTTOM OF MY HEART!
>
> At our first meeting in the Hambrick Sunday School classroom late last Winter I challenged us to think about what "success" in church-sponsored community gardening means. Well, over the past 9 months we have developed a garden, made some new friends, prayed in the garden

together, gotten to meet some of our next door neighbors and know them (and their dogs) on a first-name basis, watched an Eagle Scout complete his project and provide us with irrigation and raised beds, grew a pumpkin patch, watched children planting flowers, planted an orchard, harvested lots of tomatoes, cursed the fact that we planted so many cherry tomato plants, laughed as Jeremiah tried to prevent Eli from picking and eating so many cherry tomatoes, and experienced just how much grace there is in that there soil. I would call that a successful season.

May God bless us with many more.

Also, it's not too early to begin thinking about our Spring growing season. If you would like to be involved with Allelon Garden in 2012 please do let me know. I'd love to talk to you about it.

As I trust this email testifies, Allelon has had a positive impact in its first growing season both for me personally and corporately for Faith Baptist Church and for the Georgetown Community at large.

Yet, in thinking about the successes we enjoyed, we realize that it is also important to consider how we might continue to improve. One of the ways in which we still have great room for improvement involves inviting more of our neighbors to participate. For our first season, we only had one regular garden participant who was not a member of Faith Baptist Church; her name was Charlotte Schaut. I had met Charlotte through a Master Gardener's class that we took together and invited her to come take part in our new garden. She did, and she was one of our most consistent participants. One of my greatest memories from our first growing season involves praying with Charlotte in the middle of the garden one warm evening after she had received some bad news about her health. Sadly, Charlotte passed away in March of 2012. We are still thinking about how we are going to honor her memory and the great gift that her presence, encouragement and friendship brought to us.

CHAPTER FIVE

Cultivating Multiplication

Identifying Best Practices for Launching
a Christ-Centered Community Garden

TOWARDS THE END OF her book *City Bountiful*, Laura Lawson gestures toward some best practices for sustainable community gardening. She proposes, "For a garden to sustain itself as a community resource, three critical areas need to be addressed: balancing local and interest-based leadership, land security, and public support."[1] Although Lawson's work here highlights some of the best practices regarding the sustainability of community gardens in general, my goal is to identify more specifically from among the previous case-studies some best practices for launching Christ-centered community gardens. First, however, I will briefly explore the question as to *why* Christ-centered community gardens at all? In short, what specifically defines a Christ-centered community garden and what differentiates one from other kinds of community gardens? What is the good of Christ-centered community gardening that is distinct from other kinds of community gardening? And how do such gardens contribute

1. Lawson, *City Bountiful*, 297.

to the ongoing tradition of urban and community gardening in the United States?

I propose that a Christ-centered community garden is a piece of land farmed by a group of people who are committed to gardening together in a way that intentionally points to the person and way of Jesus Christ. The specific ways in which any individual Christ-centered community garden will point or witness towards the person and way of Christ may vary, as will the ways in which each of these gardens chooses to name their witness. Like Anathoth Community Garden, one garden might focus on the theme of gospel reconciliation and healing the wounds of physical violence in the community surrounding the garden. Other Christ-centered community gardens might choose to focus on giving food to the hungry in their town, intentionally connecting that practice with the Christ who fed the hungry multitudes according to the Gospel accounts (e.g., Luke 9:12–17, John 6:1–14, Matthew 14:13–21). Others still might choose to focus on Christ-centered community gardening as a spiritual discipline, perhaps making connections between spiritual growth and the virtues cultivated through the disciplines of gardening. Or, a Christ-centered community garden might focus on Christ's teaching about the harvest being plentiful but the laborers being few, thus using their garden as a launch pad for connecting missionally in more fruitful ways with people who live near the garden but who are otherwise disconnected from the church family.

In other words, my hope is that Christ-centered community gardening would be broad enough to encapsulate any church-sponsored (or Christian-institution sponsored) community garden that earnestly seeks to connect its garden work with its Christian mission in an ongoing way.[2] Based on my experience

2. I recognize that faith communities who do not identify with the Christian tradition but who are interested in starting a community garden would be unlikely to adopt the particular language of Christ-centered community gardening. Although it is beyond the scope of this project to investigate how community gardening might connect with the theologies and practices of different specific faith traditions, my hope would be that Jewish, Hindu, Buddhist and Muslims, for example, would be interested both in community gardening

with Allelon Community Garden, the *ongoingness* of connecting the garden to the person and way of Christ will be the most difficult part. It was relatively easy during the brainstorming days of Allelon Community Garden to say that the garden would be connected to the way of Christ in this way or that, but the reality is that, as Dr. Homer White once put it, "people do community gardening at the rump end of busy lives." Because of this, and as noted earlier in this project, the commitment level among the average community gardener is low. When life gets hectic, community gardening seems to be one of those activities that falls by the wayside for the average community gardener. Because of this reality, it would be up to the leader and the lead team (i.e., the most committed core of volunteers) of a Christ-centered community garden to ensure not only that the tomatoes still get watered in early July when half the church is away on vacation, but also that weekly or at least monthly *specific, concrete connections are being made intentionally* between the work of the gardeners and the person and way of Christ.

Not surprisingly, these kinds of intentional connections between a community garden and the person and work of Christ distinguishes Christ-centered community gardens from other kinds of community gardens. Yet, without question most of the goods of community gardening in general (the therapeutic benefits, beautification, exercise, etc.) also prevail for Christ-centered community gardening. Thus, one might think of Christ-centered community gardening as a kind of artistic riff on more traditional forms of urban and community gardening. Indeed, Christ-centered community gardening descends from and creatively continues the traditions and iterations of urban and community gardening in the United States over the last century.

Although all three of the gardens highlighted in the case-studies above are sponsored by a Church or a Christian college, none of them were created with a thick *a priori* conception of what a Christ-centered community garden might be. Rather, my sense is that the garden leaders from each of the three respective gardens

---

and in articulating how the work of community gardening connects with their faith and practices.

began with a strong sense that community gardening connected with their understanding of spiritual disciplines and Christian witness to the world. All three sensed that God's timing was at work and that the formation of their garden connected to a specific need present in their respective communities at that time. From those origins each garden has been moving forward, making unexpected discoveries about how their community gardening efforts have connected to their faith and their neighborhoods, naming those discoveries as they emerge.

What follows is the culmination of the work of this project, a listing of fifteen best practices that I have identified for launching a Christ-centered community garden. They are listed chronologically starting with the earliest stages of launching a Christ-centered community garden.

Fifteen Best Practices for Launching a Christ-Centered Community Garden

1. *Pray for discernment*

2. *Share the vision of the garden with others in order to recruit a team of people who are committed to working in the garden for the first year*

   - intentionally strive to recruit people of different generations

3. *Have an identifiable group of people (a "lead team") behind the project before approaching the powers-that-be regarding permission to use some land to start the garden*

4. *Intentionally ask for the input and insights of others during every step of the garden-launching process*

   - strive for participatory and deliberative decision-making

5. *Rather than asking the powers-that-be for money for the garden, plan for the garden to be* **budget neutral**

   - secure and be prepared to articulate other revenue/fundraising streams

6. *Before meeting with the powers-that-be, already have a few different places for potential garden plots in mind (with plans for water-sourcing)*

   - be open to their ideas regarding garden placement and water-sourcing

7. *With your team, decide whether your garden will consist of individual plots, a community plot, or both*

8. *With your team, decide whether you will garden organically or not*

   - once that decision is made, be prepared to explain to others why your team chose whichever of those options you chose

9. *Connect with a local farm from whom you can buy compost and mulch in bulk*

10. *Decide in advance if your community garden will require participants to sign a partner agreement form and if there will be an annual fee*

11. *Once decisions have been made about the partner agreement form and some kind of brochure or card for the garden has been created, go door-to-door and invite neighbors to participate in the garden*

12. *Plan a service of consecration/dedication for the garden around the time you first break ground*

    - invite pastor/lay leaders to help lead the service

13. *Plan to meet monthly either in person (perhaps for a potluck lunch, ideally serving food from the garden when feasible) or at least over email to have conversations and make decisions about the garden*

14. *Brainstorm intentional things to keep Christ at the center of your church-sponsored community garden*

    - this focus can be easy to lose: some ideas include integrating gardening themes into preaching series and small group studies that the church sponsors, short devotions at the beginning of group garden work, prayer in the garden, etc.

15. *Once you begin harvesting produce, give away some of it to the congregation or sponsoring organization, encourage garden partners to take some of it home with them for personal consumption, go door-to-door giving away some of it to the garden's neighbors ("free farmer's market"), and give away the rest of the produce (and there should be plenty left!) to your local food bank for the hungry*

Resources for Further Reflection

Website for the American Community Garden Association: https://communitygarden.org/

Abi-Nader, Jeanette, Kendall Dunnigan, and Kristen Markely. *Growing Communities Curriculum*. Philadelphia: American Community Gardening Association, 2001.

Bartholomew, Mel. *All New Square Foot Gardening: Grow More in Less Space!* Revised Edition ed. Nashville, Tenn.: Cool Springs Press, 2006.

Berry, Wendell. *Bringing It to the Table: On Farming and Food*. Later printing ed. Berkeley, CA: Counterpoint, 2009.

Davis, Ellen. *Scripture, Culture, and Agriculture: An Agrarian Reading of the Bible*. Cambridge: Cambridge University Press, 2009.

Derrida, Jacques and Anne Dufourmantelle. *Of Hospitality*. Stanford, Calif.: Stanford University Press, 2000.

Helphand, Kenneth I. *Defiant Gardens: Making Gardens in Wartime*. San Antonio, TX: Trinity University Press, 2008.

Houtan, Kyle S. Van. *Diversity and Dominion: Dialogues in Ecology, Ethics, and Theology*. Edited by Kyle S. Van Houtan and Michael S. Northcott. Eugene, OR: Pickwick Publications, 2010.

Jackson, Wes. *Consulting the Genius of the Place: An Ecological Approach to a New Agriculture*. 1St Edition ed. Berkeley, CA: Counterpoint, 2010.

Kingsolver, Barbara, Camille Kingsolver, and Steven L. Hopp. *Animal, Vegetable, Miracle: A Year of Food Life (P.S.)*. New York: Harper Perennial, 2008.

Kinnaman, David. *You Lost Me: Why Young Christians are Leaving Church...and Rethinking Faith*. Grand Rapids, MI: Baker Books, 2011.

Moschella, Mary Clark. *Ethnography As A Pastoral Practice: An Introduction*. Cleveland, OH: The Pilgrim Press, 2008.

Pollan, Michael. *Second Nature: A Gardener's Education*. New York, NY.: Grove Press, 2003.

Pollan, Michael. *The Omnivore's Dilemma: A Natural History of Four Meals*. Reprint ed. New York: Penguin, 2007.

Pratt, Lonni Collins, and Father Daniel Homan. *Radical Hospitality: Benedict's Way of Love, 2nd Edition*. Brewster, Mass.: Paraclete Press, 2011.

Russell, Letty M. *Just Hospitality: God's Welcome in a World of Difference*. Edited by J. Shannon Clarkson and Kate M. Ott. Louisville, KY.: Westminster John Knox, 2009.

Sutherland, Arthur. *I Was a Stranger: a Christian Theology of Hospitality*. Nashville: Abingdon Press, 2006.

Wirzba, Norman. *Food and Faith: a Theology of Eating*. New York: Cambridge University Press, 2011.

————. *The Paradise of God: Renewing Religion in an Ecological Age.*Oxford: Oxford University Press, 2003.

Wirzba, Norman, ed. *The Essential Agrarian Reader: The Future of Culture, Community, and the Land*. Washington D.C.: Shoemaker and Hoard, 2004.

Appendix

Faith Community Garden Proposal
A Conversation Re-Initiated by the New, Yet-to-be-Named Sunday Morning Small Group

Presented by Bryan Langlands

Why start a community garden at Faith?

1. *As a vehicle for missions and outward focus*

    - By inviting the church building's most immediate neighbors to participate in the garden, we will gain opportunities to meet and build relationships with new friends.

    - We would give much of the harvest from the garden to the Amen House.

2. *As a teaching tool*

- Our Children's Ministry and Youth Ministry could use the garden to teach young people about the Gospel (think about how many of Jesus' parables have to do with seeds, soil, harvest, etc.!), about creation care, healthy eating, ethical eating, etc.

3. *As an opportunity for intergenerational ministry*

- As ministry is becoming increasingly separated by age groups, a garden is a great place for different generations to work together and to learn from one another. It also provides an opportunity for skilled gardeners to teach beginners.

4. *As a source for summer potluck lunches*

- Fresh, healthy food that would be as local as you can get.

First Step: Education and Dialogue – February/March

A few important points

- The garden would be budget neutral. A new account would be created for the garden and the Garden Leadership Team (see below) would be responsible for doing the fundraising needed to supply the garden's needs.

- The garden would be located on the vacant lots behind the church building. The hope is that the garden would allow us to connect in new ways with our neighbors in Bradford Place and in Hunter Ridge.

- Even though the soil on these lots may not be ideal, we would spend time improving the soil and use raised beds where needed. Part of the goal of church sponsored community-gardening involves the good that comes from the process of preparing the soil and gardening, not just the end product.

Second Step: Planning – March/April

a. Interested members will be invited to join a Garden Leadership Team that will begin meeting weekly (at first) in order to make the decisions needed in order to launch the garden. This Team will then be the group who is responsible and accountable to the church's leadership for the garden's activities.

b. Questions that this Team will need to decide will include: How specifically would this garden connect with the mission of Faith Baptist Church? How could the garden become a tool for outreach to the church building's most immediate neighbors? Would the garden be organic or not (and why or why not)? How would we get water to the garden? Would the garden consist of individual plots or would it all be communally gardened? If there are individual plots, could Sunday School classes adopt a plot and/or connect with neighbors in Bradford Place or Hunter Ridge to take care of a plot? Could we start a composting program in the Church that would both recycle food and coffee scraps and provide free fertilizer/soil enhancer for our garden? What would we name the garden?

c. Going door-to-door to talk to neighbors in Bradford Place and Hunter Ridge about the Garden and opportunities for getting involved.

Third Step: Preparing the Soil and/or Creating Raised Beds – March/April

Fourth Step: Planting – March/April/May

Bibliography

Hershberger, Michele. *A Christian View of Hospitality: Expecting Surprises.* Scottdale, Pa.: Herald Pr, 1999.

Koenig, John. *New Testament Hospitality: Partnership with Strangers as Promise and Mission.* Eugene, OR: Wipf & Stock Publishers, 2001.

Lawson, Laura J. *City Bountiful: A Century of Community Gardening in America.* Berkeley: University of California Press, 2005.

Newman, Elizabeth. *Untamed Hospitality: Welcoming God and Other Strangers.* Grand Rapids, Mich.: Brazos Press, 2007.

Nouwen, Henri J.M. *Reaching Out: the Three Movements of the Spiritual Life.* Garden City, N.Y.: Image, 1986.

Oden, Amy G. *God's Welcome: Hospitality For a Gospel-Hungry World.* Cleveland, Ohio.: Pilgrim Press, 2008.

Pohl, Christine D. *Making Room: Recovering Hospitality as a Christian Tradition.* Grand Rapids, Mich.: William B. Eerdmans Publishing Company, 1999.

Westerhoff, Caroline. *Good Fences: The Boundaries of Hospitality.* Harrisburg, Pa.: Morehouse Publishing, 2004.

Williams, Roger. "Mr. Cotton's Letter Lately Printed, Examined and Answered." 1644.

www.ingramcontent.com/pod-product-compliance
Lightning Source LLC
Chambersburg PA
CBHW070502090426
42735CB00012B/2652